P9-DTI-720

IMPROVING BOARD EFFECTIVENESS

PRACTICAL LESSONS FOR NONPROFIT HEALTH CARE ORGANIZATIONS

THOMAS P. HOLLAND, PhD

ROGER A. RITVO, PhD

ANTHONY R. KOVNER, PhD

WITHDRAWN
UTSA LIBRARIES

AMERICAN HOSPITAL PUBLISHING, INC.
AN AMERICAN HOSPITAL ASSOCIATION COMPANY
CHICAGO

PUBLISHED IN COOPERATION WITH:

 NEHA
New England Healthcare Assembly

This publication is designed to provide accurate and authoritative information in regard to the subject matter covered. It is sold with the understanding that neither the authors nor the publisher is engaged in rendering legal, accounting, or other professional service. If legal advice or other expert assistance is required, the services of a competent professional person should be sought.

The views expressed in this publication are strictly those of the authors and do not necessarily represent official positions of the American Hospital Association or the New England Healthcare Assembly.

Library of Congress Cataloging-in-Publication Data

Holland, Thomas P.
    Improving board effectiveness : practical lessons for nonprofit
health care organizations / Thomas P. Holland, Roger A. Ritvo,
Anthony R. Kovner.
      p.   cm.
    Includes bibliographical references and index.
    ISBN 1-55648-181-0
    1. Health services administration. 2. Hospital trustees.
3. Nonprofit organizations—Management. I. Ritvo, Roger A., 1944–
II. Kovner, Anthony R. III. Title.
    [DNLM: 1. Governing Board—organization & administration.
2. Hospital Administration—methods. 3. Health Services—
—organization & administration. 4. Organizations, Nonprofit—
—organization & administration. WX 150 H737i 1997]
    RA971.H57 1997
    362.1′068—dc21
    DNLM/DLC
    for Library of Congress
                               96-49002
                                 CIP

Catalog no. 196113

All rights reserved. The reproduction or use of this book in any form or in any information storage or retrieval system is forbidden without the express written permission of the publisher.

Printed in the USA

© 1997 by American Hospital Publishing, Inc., an American Hospital Association company.

AHA is a service mark of the American Hospital Association used under license by American Hospital Publishing, Inc.

Cover design by Jeanne Calabrese Design

Discounts on bulk quantities of books published by American Hospital Publishing, Inc. (AHPI), are available to professional associations, special marketers, educators, trainers, and others. For details and discount information contact:
American Hospital Publishing, Inc.
Books Division
737 North Michigan Avenue
Chicago, Illinois 60611-2615 FAX 312/951-8491

Thomas P. Holland

> To my wife, Myra Blackmon, for her continuous support and encouragement as well as thoughtful questions and suggestions throughout this wonderful journey together.

Roger A. Ritvo

> To my mother and father, Mikki and Mike Ritvo, who devoted their lives to service and helping others.

Anthony R. Kovner

> To my wife, Christine Tassone Kovner, from whom I am continually learning about really governing.

Contents

List of Figures vi

About the Authors vii

Preface ix

Acknowledgments xi

Chapter 1. Getting Started on Performance Improvement 1

Chapter 2. Taking Initial Steps toward Change 9

Chapter 3. Building Instrumental Competencies 17

Chapter 4. Building Social Competencies 29

Chapter 5. Assessing Performance and Identifying Targets
          for Change 39

Chapter 6. Holding Retreats for Board Development 49

Chapter 7. Setting Goals for Action 59

Chapter 8. Examining Three Models of Governance 65

Chapter 9. Sustaining Ongoing Improvement Initiatives 75

Chapter 10. Case Studies and Discussion Questions 79

Appendix. Board Self-Assessment Questionnaire 87

Reference List 97

Index 105

List of Figures

Figure 5-1. Board Meeting Evaluation Form 41

Figure 5-2. Sample Annual Board Evaluation Form.............. 44

Figure 5-3. Sample Assessment of Board Member
Performance 45

Figure 6-1. Sample Board Retreat Plan 52

Figure 6-2. Sample Discussion Questions 56

Figure 7-1. Examples of Board Goals in Three
Organizations 61

Figure 7-2. Framework for Monitoring Progress
on Board Goals 62

About the Authors

Thomas P. Holland, PhD, is professor and director of the Kellogg Project on Effective Governance, University of Georgia School of Social Work. He also holds an appointment as clinical professor in the department of psychiatry and health behavior, Medical College of Georgia. He received his PhD from Brandeis University, where his studies focused on the management of nonprofit organizations. Dr. Holland has taught, conducted research, and provided consultation in this field for over 30 years. He is currently developing a new interdisciplinary graduate program on leadership of nonprofit organizations. Dr. Holland designed the board assessment format described later in this book, and he is the author of numerous other publications on governance, including *How to Build a Better Board*. Along with colleagues, Richard Chait and Barbara Taylor, he also authored *The Effective Board of Trustees, Improving the Performance of Governing Boards,* and "The New Work of the Nonprofit Board" (*Harvard Business Review,* Sept. 1996).

Roger A. Ritvo, PhD, MBA, is dean and professor of health management and policy at the School of Health and Human Services of the University of New Hampshire. He holds a PhD in organizational behavior and development from Case Western Reserve University and an MBA in health services administration from George Washington University. He has served as a visiting scholar at Sheffield University in England, a visiting professor at American University, and as assistant dean for 10 years at Case Western Reserve University. Dr. Ritvo received the "Outstanding Administrator Award" from the University of New Hampshire's student government and the "Certificate of Merit" from its Women's Commission. Dr. Ritvo has also served on numerous boards of directors, including the NTL Institute for Applied Behavioral Science, Health and Human Service, Inc. (a Catholic multi-hospital system), the Cleveland Arthritis Foundation, and his temple. He consults public and private organizations in the health, human service, and corporate sectors. He has edited four books, contributed chapters in six volumes, written numerous articles, book reviews, and editorial pieces and has made frequent appearances on radio talk and news shows. Dr. Ritvo's recent book, *Managing in the Age of Change,* has received praise from practitioners in both the profit and nonprofit sectors. He is currently working on *Sisters in Sorrow,* biographies of prisoners who served as doctors and nurses in the Nazi concentration camps. He has been listed in *Who's Who* for a decade.

Anthony R. Kovner, PhD, is professor of health policy and management at the Robert F. Wagner Graduate School of Public Service at New York University and a member of the Board of Trustees of the Lutheran Medical Center of Brooklyn, NY. He has extensively consulted in the health care field in areas of board development, management development, implementation of community benefit programs, and strategic planning. An experienced health care manager, he has served as CEO of a community hospital, senior health care consultant for a large industrial union, and as a manager of a group practice, a nursing home, and a large ambulatory care services program. Dr. Kovner is the author or coauthor of numerous books and articles. His books include *Really Managing, Really Trying: A Career Guide for the Health Services Manager, Health Care Delivery in the United States* (which has sold over 170,000 copies), *The Role of the Physician Executive, Health Services Management: Readings and Commentary,* and *Health Services Management: A Book of Cases.* His article, "Improving Hospital Board Effectiveness: An Update" (*Frontiers of Health Services Management,* Spring 1990), was chosen as the outstanding Healthcare Article of the Year in 1990 by the American College of Healthcare Executives.

Preface

This book emerged from the authors' collaboration on a five-year action research intervention funded by the W. K. Kellogg Foundation. In this and a related project, we worked closely with the boards of diverse non-profit organizations, several of which were hospitals and community health promotion organizations. Our objective was to explore how boards went about improving on their performance. We sought to identify lessons and practices that could be used by boards of other organizations wanting to strengthen their own effectiveness.

This book is addressed primarily to executives and board members of nonprofit hospitals and health care organizations. We emphasize the experiences of those health care boards that participated in these projects as well as numerous other health care organizations where we have provided consultation and training. Their collective examples offer invaluable guidance for boards of other similar entities that want to improve their performance.

Among our most important conclusions from these projects, as well as from our ongoing work with boards of numerous other organizations, is that the lessons described in this book apply throughout the nonprofit and health sectors. Although most organizations see themselves as unique in many ways, all share basic challenges related to performance quality and effectiveness. The essential ingredients of effective governance are generic, and the experiences of boards that have made changes that strengthened their performance serve as valuable guides to other boards desiring to do better.

Even though boards need not necessarily be involved in a multi-year project with outside consultants to do better work, it is essential that they devote sustained attention to their own performance if improvements are to be realized. For any team aspiring to higher performance levels, reflecting on the group experiences and practicing new approaches are necessary activities for achieving change. To assist such efforts, this book is organized to address a number of key concerns raised by executives and board members seeking to add value that their boards contribute to the organization. Benchmarking not only allows us to draw from best practices among the many boards we have encountered, it provides valuable examples for others to follow.

In response to the question "What are we supposed to be doing as a board?" we begin with a description of the basic responsibilities and duties of governing boards. We describe some ideals of governance and explore symptoms that indicate board underperformance. Then we identify some of the experiences—problems *and* opportunities—that attract a board's attention to its own performance and invite planned changes for improving the quality of its service.

In response to the question "How can we get to work on improving our performance?" we describe a range of assessment tools and methods boards have used to identify specific targets for change. Six distinct skill areas of highly effective boards are presented, accompanied by questions a board can use to self-evaluate in each area and identify possible steps toward improvement.

Next we discuss the benefit of retreats as a method for concentrated work on board development, as well as other approaches boards have used to install changes that facilitated more effective performance. Case studies drawn from our experience with various boards illustrate core issues trustees face and practical steps for addressing them. Finally, we summarize some of the best practices effective boards use to sustain ongoing improvements in their performance quality.

Acknowledgments

Thanks to the generous financial support of the W. K. Kellogg Foundation, with its long history of commitment to quality improvement among health care organizations and services worldwide, we had the unusual opportunity to spend extensive time with participating boards. We especially appreciate the support and encouragement of Robert DeVries, our project officer at the foundation.

Parallel to this project, Tom Holland also worked with colleagues Richard P. Chait and Barbara E. Taylor on a similar study of governing boards of private liberal arts colleges. Findings from those sites enriched our reflections on boards of other types of nonprofit organizations. We are especially grateful for the wise counsel and insights of Dick and Barbara, as well as many other colleagues who study and work with nonprofit boards.

We are indebted also to Douglas Jackson, who served as our research assistant, and to Martha Lund, our administrative assistant, for their extensive efforts on behalf of this project. Finally, we express our deep gratitude to Liz Kramer, consultant to the New England Healthcare Assembly, and to those trustees and executives who participated in the project. Though they must remain anonymous, we have highlighted their experiences and lessons throughout this book. They would be pleased to know that others benefited from their courageous examples.

Chapter 1

Getting Started on Performance Improvement

Health care organizations operate in an increasingly complex and demanding environment. Their survival is challenged by extensive changes in public policies, funding patterns, technological innovations, labor force characteristics, community attitudes and expectations, and competitor actions. Federal policy changes during the early Reagan years that established Diagnosis-Related Groups (DRGs) pushed health care organizations to learn the language of business. This led to a dramatic growth in for-profit health care corporations, which introduced competition with traditional nonprofit organizations ("nonprofits"). Tax code changes limiting the related services that nonprofits could own led to establishment of the wholly owned subsidiary, a new corporate structure for the traditional hospital.

Concurrent with these public policy changes was the growing need among large corporations to control escalating costs for their employee health benefits. Corporate demands for cost control pressured health care organizations to exercise tighter measures on the expansion and delivery of their services. Boards of nonprofit health care organizations began using strategies borrowed from the business sector—strategies such as mergers, consolidations, acquisitions, shared facilities, and closures.

Extensive attention directed to health care services during the 1992 presidential campaign further fueled these changes. The national concern for reform was strong, though it did not result in the broad, single-payer system advocates pushed for. Growth of health maintenance organizations and other managed care approaches has accelerated; many formerly nonprofit organizations, such as Blue Cross, have moved to become for-profit corporations.

Changes such as these have placed enormous burdens on nonprofit health care organizations. Responding effectively to these challenges requires every system component—*including trustee boards*—to operate at maximum strength and productivity. Although health care staff and management have implemented many practice changes geared toward performance betterment, their boards often have not kept pace with improvement efforts. Boards that *have* taken initiatives provide more effective governance and leadership, thereby guiding their organizations into positions of strength and situating them for future growth.

Understanding Issues Related to Board Effectiveness

Trustee boards must expedite their work in new and different ways to meet the increasingly stringent legal mandates and social imperatives placed on them and the organizations they govern. Many new resources lend support to improvement initiatives; for example, a variety of conferences, such as the New England Healthcare Assembly and the Association of Governing Boards, consultants, and publications (Bowen, 1994; Carver, 1991; and Houle, 1989) offer guidance on how to improve the quality of board performance.

Team Development

Many resources emphasize the benefits of self-directed work teams and associated skills. Board members who approach their work with a team mind-set consistently report the following advantages:

- Stronger sense of commitment to, and ownership of, their final products
- More frequent interactions with parties beyond boardroom colleagues
- More informed decision making
- Higher productivity
- Deeper satisfaction with their contributions to the organization

Most important, effective teams function as models throughout the organization. They demonstrate by example how ongoing improvements in work quality can be effected.

Such results do not occur by accident. Meaningful team development takes time to implement, energy to support, and resources to maintain. Education and orientation are essential prerequisites for effective board service. To build valuable teams, boards must cultivate specific skills:

- Strategic planning
- Full grasp of organization mission and its context
- Establishment and maintenance of critical linkages with the external community

- Critical analysis of issues
- Interpersonal and communication skills

Partnership Development and a Focus on Mission

Boards can help or hinder organizational management. If the governance team and each managing team forge strong and skilled partnerships for carrying out their duties, the organization can achieve its potential. A basic function of a board–management partnership is to maintain focus on the institution's mission. Central questions are "What is our purpose?" and "How should we carry it out in the years ahead?"

Keeping the mission in view and formulating a well-delineated strategy for moving toward it provide the entire organization with a sense of direction. Policies emerge from the mission and vision, in turn guiding choices and organizationwide priorities. Ultimately, because these choices and priorities become targets for resource allocation, budgets represent system priorities and system values. Identifying criteria for monitoring movement toward goals and applying these criteria to assess performance allows everyone to witness the organization's (and the board's) resource accountability.

Linkage and Philosophy

Ensuring that the right governance skills and partnerships are in place is crucial to effective leadership. However, almost anyone who has served on a board occasionally has left a meeting wondering *why* he or she accepted the responsibility in the first place. Problems can seem complex; frustration can run high; meetings feel almost palpably overburdened with issues and distressingly meager in results. Ambiguous connection between problems, board energies, resource allocation, and service outcomes often are due to few boards understanding how to educate members and prepare them to carry out their duties effectively. Merely attending meetings and voting on recommendations fall far from realistic requirements in today's health care environment.

Most trustees begin their service with high ideals about their role and their organization's purpose, only to become unmoored by conflicting philosophies. For example, while some trustees are content with old practices, others wonder what they can do to help the board dispatch its duties more productively. Their motivation is to add value to the organization and maximize contributions to the accomplishment of organization mission. Unfortunately, they do not know *how* to achieve that goal and, as a result, resort to the more familiar territory of operations management. The result is a philosophical gap that steers board attention away from the tougher questions surrounding the organization's future.

Governance versus Administration

Directing attention to board quality and effectiveness can be a challenging, if ambiguous, process at the outset. For one thing, the majority of members may accept board practices and customs with little questioning. Also, as already indicated, many boards lapse into focusing on administrative matters rather than governance issues. Despite advice to avoid trying to micro-manage the organization, too many boards spend their time and energy second-guessing management decisions. Hard at work on the wrong things, they provide little real governance. Some wonder how, as part-time amateurs, they can be of any real help to full-time executive experts; nevertheless they keep seeking opportunities to contribute "something of value" to the proceedings.

Changing old habits and customs is difficult, but many boards have found a number of useful tools and procedures to assist their initiatives to govern more effectively. Likewise, helpful resources from national associations can further aid these steps. This book describes some of the methods and strategies boards have used to work on improving their effectiveness. The practices discussed have led to more productive meetings, greater value added to the organization, and higher trustee satisfaction with quality of their work. To provide a context for considering more effective practices, the following section briefly recounts basic board responsibilities and key challenges in carrying out trustee roles.

Understanding Basic Board Responsibilities

Nonprofit hospitals and health care organizations are expressions of a distinctive Western tradition, having grown from early charitable and religious refuges for the sick and suffering in our communities. They are driven by the mission to provide treatment for the ill and promote community health. Like other nonprofit organizations, many of the services they provide would be problematic in the for-profit marketplace. For one thing, people frequently distrust a profit motive behind caring for the sick; also, a number of health care program benefits are collective and therefore difficult to evaluate quantitatively. Nevertheless, these organizations must run efficiently while providing optimal service quality.

Further complicating this picture are differences in accountability: Whereas public organizations are accountable to taxpayers and private businesses to shareholders, nonprofits are governed by self-perpetuating trustee boards. The traditional assumption is that these boards represent the interests of their communities and constituencies; in recent years, however, numerous reports claiming neglect of duties have undermined this public trust. Even so, many boards continue to *underscrutinize* their performance, further jeopardizing community trust.

The work of a nonprofit board has been described as carrying out "responsible community ownership" (Umbdenstock, 1992). Like their counterparts in other nonprofit organizations, hospital and health system boards are responsible for several basic functions:

- They select, support, advise, and evaluate the CEO and, if necessary, replace this person.
- They review and adopt long-term strategic directions for the organization and obtain or allocate financial resources to carry them out.
- They ensure that the necessary human and financial resources are available to pursue organization goals and objectives related to providing essential community services.
- They monitor management's performance and seek to ensure that the organization operates responsibly and effectively.
- They assume responsibility for selecting new members and establishing an effective system of governance. This includes regular evaluation of board performance and systematic education of members for carrying out their duties (Bowen, 1994).

Most hospital trustees are familiar with the CEO selection process and the nomination and approval process for new board members. These tasks are widely assumed by stakeholders to "belong to" the board rather than any other group. Of course, organization stakeholders (such as the medical staff) attempt to influence trustee decisions, but final word generally rests with the board.

Most boards also review the organization's strategic directions and ensure that the necessary financial and human resources are in place to carry them out. This review process varies among boards. For example, a Planning Committee and a Finance Committee may be charged with this responsibility. Usually, Planning Committees are involved in decisions to initiate or close services, whereas Finance Committees address capital, operating funds, cash flow, and budget issues.

Even though these basic functions are vital to organizational well-being, many boards falter in exercising them. Usually they fail to:

- Establish clear and specific organizational directions, relying instead on the administration to choose and implement appropriate goals
- Ensure that the necessary resources are available to carry out those directions
- Clarify board goals, expectations, and assessment criteria for executive or organizationwide performance, resulting in the board's inability to monitor performance or ensure responsible organizational operations

- Be prepared (or willing) to evaluate its own performance or iden- tify ways to increase its value added to the organization

A number of symptoms signal when a board may be functioning below levels needed to provide effective governance. To identify these symptoms, each trustee should address at least three core questions:

1. _Does the board routinely accept committee and administrative recom- mendations, or does it vigorously analyze key issues facing the organi- zation?_ Effective boards actively engage in identifying relevant issues facing the organization, analyzing alternative responses, and setting priorities for action. Listening passively to weighty reports and voting on foregone conclusions hardly adds value to an organization. Although reports can provide useful back- ground information, trustees can read these _outside_ the boardroom, leaving more time for discussing and analyzing unresolved problems, examining alternative directions, and iden- tifying and exploring key issues and challenges the organization faces.

2. _Are board committees like separate fiefdoms digging into operational mat- ters, or are they closely linked to and clearly based on an agreed-upon strategic plan?_ Standing committees that only mirror the organi- zation's administrative structure invite forays into operational details and second-guessing management decisions. To add value to the organization, the board should design committees around key goals of the strategic plan, rather than following administra- tive divisions. Each committee or work group should be charged with a cluster of essential tasks needed to carry forward its part of the overall plan. Each group should keep the larger board informed of its actions and involved in problem solving along the way.

3. _Do newcomers sit passively, trying to discern the game rules and expec- tations of board service, or are they shown clearly and up front where and how their talents are to be directed?_ Many trustees report that they had to "learn by osmosis" what was expected of them—a practice that leaves newcomers to "figure out" how to participate productively in board work. Effective boards take the initiative to orient new members fully to board expectations, norms, and practices, and they provide mentors to help newcomers learn the participation ropes.

New members bring an invaluable resource that many boards neglect. Because they are not immersed in the history and assumptions that other members share, newcomers can question old assumptions and offer ideas about optional approaches to board work. By "standing outside the box," they can introduce fresh perspectives to problem analysis. Integrating new members into the team early on and drawing on their pristine insights can help boards find creative approaches to challenges.

Aside from showing symptoms of underperformance, many boards suffer from uncertainty over how to create and sustain an effective governance system for their organization. Trustees who remain unclear about what *specific* value they add to the organization cannot demonstrate accountability for their use of resources. Because expectations and performance assessment criteria are ambiguous, it is also unclear what can be done to develop members' skills and strengthen group performance. Individual members may have concerns about the board's effectiveness but are unsure what to do about them.

It is dangerous to allow these obscurities and discontents to go unaddressed. All nonprofit organizations depend on stakeholder trust and support for survival. When communities had fewer health care provider choices and less information about performance standards or alternative sources of care, a health care system could weather doubts about its performance. Those days are gone forever. More consumer awareness of standards and health care choices (including comparison criteria), more demanding expectations, and stepped-up competition among providers leave little room for dissatisfaction or marginal performance. Indicators of health status have not kept pace with the fact that more money is being spent on health care. Reports of incompetent performance, conflicts of interest, and excessive compensation further erode public trust. Put simply, consumer loyalty is more difficult to attain and sustain than it is to undermine.

Many health care organization boards struggle with these challenges. Others have addressed them and created very effective governance systems. Their experiences provide ideas and practices presented in subsequent chapters. Other boards can examine and adapt these practices to their own situations. We begin with some approaches that can help trustees initiate discussion about their performance, building on familiar events in the life of any organization. We also examine tools and techniques boards have used to specify performance aspects that members can work on as a team. After exploring procedures for carrying out this work and identifying important executive and board leadership tasks that promote effectiveness and performance improvement, we describe practices of high-performance boards and ways aspiring boards can self-assess performance in key governance skills. Finally, we consider strategic approaches to incorporating continuous effectiveness improvement as an element of everyday board work.

Chapter 2

Taking Initial Steps toward Change

Most trustees report having learned their roles simply by watching and listening to other trustees. As newcomers they hesitated to question or criticize what they observed, and came to accept customary practices as "normal" and beyond question.

The inherent risk in this approach is that new members come to accept long-standing practice patterns and, in doing so, perpetuate outmoded and out-of-touch board proceedings. This consequence, coupled with insufficient information about alternative practices, can deter change initiatives. It is awkward for anyone to step back from business as usual and identify aspects that might be improved—especially if the agenda is already full and time is limited. Newcomers avoid asking "naive or foolish" questions, or second-guessing what their more seasoned colleagues seem to take for granted. Furthermore, many are reluctant to question practices or conclusions without being prepared to offer a better alternative. As a result, many trustees are dissatisfied with board performance but at a loss for how to spotlight aspects that need improvement.

Several avenues offer ways for boards to begin strengthening performance levels:

- Pausing after successful completion of a difficult task or project to identify and discuss what led to success
- Taking advantage of natural breaks or events in routine business to examine the board's role leading to the situation and how it might handle such events more effectively in the future
- Expanding the organization's accountability obligations and practices to the board
- Translating members' expressions of discontent with board performance into group commitments for action
- Responding to leadership initiatives to change and improve aspects of the board's work

These approaches are not mutually exclusive; a board may use several of them simultaneously. Effective movement through any of these approaches rests on board leaders opening discussions to the entire membership and supporting group efforts to identify specific targets for change. The following sections examine these avenues more closely.

Taking Advantage of Natural Events

Certain events or turning points throughout an organization's life invite opportunity to reexamine the board's role. For example, successful completion of a major campaign, emergence of a problem or challenge, a break in routine, or a situation that interrupts business as usual lends itself to reflection. By examining how the board contributed to successes, problems, or missed opportunities, trustees can formulate ways to deal more effectively with similar situations in the future.

Retrospective study also can disclose advantageous (or disadvantageous) actions, steps, or skills that led to success or further challenge. Learning from experience—celebrating victories and turning failure into opportunities—stirs trustee awareness of individual and collective performance.

The board also may be challenged by a discovery of changes in another organization that provides competing services to the public or that gives that organization access to an important resource (such as patient referrals or awards granted). Expressions of dissatisfaction or confrontations with key constituents (for example, staff unrest or contract disputes with outside organizations) also signal potential opportunities for the board to assess its role in the situation as well as the administration's role. More extreme occurrences include transition under a new CEO or discovery of a violation of trust—for example, breach of ethics or law (such as embezzlement of funds) by an agent of the organization. Less extreme breaks include turnover in board leadership or questions about board composition, membership, or service.

In addition to addressing *consequential issues* accompanying these situations, the board should also reflect on *contributory issues* resulting from its own role in emergence of a problem. Members might make use of discussion questions such as these:

- How did we allow ourselves to get into this situation? What clues did we miss?
- What should we do to prevent such oversights in the future?
- What steps can we take to work together more effectively in the months ahead?

Newcomers can ask questions about practices taken for granted: "Why do we always do this? Why not try that?" Or, "What business should we *really* be in?" Or, "How should we approach this new market in light of the organization's mission?" Changes in availability of services from competitors or concerns about mergers or acquisitions may stimulate discussions of alternative trade-offs between mission and market, leading to further reflection on the board's role in addressing such issues.

Successes and challenges such as these occur in any organization's experience and invite the board to consider its own actions and contributions to the larger organization in ways that seem neither forced nor artificial. They offer opportunities to assess how the board performed during the period leading up to this point, how its actions (or inactions) may have contributed to the present situation, and how it could change its practices to become more effective in dealing with such matters in the future. In addition to working directly on the problem itself, the board can take advantage of the situation to consider how it might dispatch its role more effectively to add greater value to the organization.

A number of boards already use executive or board leadership transitions to consider the organization's recent performance and the future challenges it is likely to face. Discussing these issues can lead to formulation of candidate assessment criteria. They also can help trustees define the board's work for the coming year.

A natural extension of such reflections is evaluation of board performance in recent years and its contributions to successes and problems of the outgoing leader. Often such discussions reveal ambiguities in performance goals, expectations, or criteria. They may expose divergent perceptions of market or mission that gave mixed signals to the executive and even among trustees. This kind of assessment is vital if the board is to provide stronger leadership and a more effective partnership with the incoming executive.

By directing attention to the board's direct role in situations, trustees and directors can learn what to do (or do differently) to contribute more effectively to future success of new leaders.

Even without a major change in leadership, the board can periodically request the executive to talk candidly about challenges the organization will face in the coming months or years. Then the group can explore ways to strengthen partnership with the executive so as to prepare for those challenges.

Current trustees can make thoughtful use of newcomers' questions about board practices, assumptions, or priorities to reflect on its customary activities and alternatives. For example, they can take advantage of questions about competing priorities (such as market versus mission) or the feasibility of launching a capital campaign as occasions to examine how well the board has dealt with past challenges and how it could change its practices to become more effective in the future. In sum, the board can embrace any substantive turning point or organizational challenge as an opportunity to learn how to improve its own performance.

Extending Accountability to Include the Board

Many boards periodically review how the organization and its managers deal with accountability issues. Such questions might arise during reviews of recent financial performance and discussions of proposed annual budgets. These occasions provide another natural avenue to evaluating board performance. Accountability discussions can be expanded to include the board by asking the following questions:

- How does this board add value to the organization beyond that added by the administration?
- How does the board demonstrate accountability for its use of time and resources?
- What steps can the board take to improve its accountability and communicate that improvement to others?

Every board has a vital governance responsibility to ensure that the organization is sustaining public trust and goodwill by demonstrating its responsible and efficient use of all resources. It is appropriate for boards to expect the executive to provide information by which trustees can monitor various aspects of organizational performance, finances, and outcomes on a regular basis. After all, the board holds administration and staff accountable for their use of organization resources. The auditor's annual "management letter" also may single out issues for the CEO and board to consider, such as record keeping, changes in standard accounting practices, separating financial matters from medical matters, or financial reserves. It is a natural step to broaden these healthy expectations to include the board.

The trustee board can extend its familiar accountability practices by directing attention to the ways it is — or could be — demonstrating accountability for its own actions and resource utilization. Discussions might begin with identifying how and where the board adds value to the organization, beyond that contributed by administration and staff. Then members can explore ways to use time, skills, and other resources more effectively to strengthen the quality of its contributions. After selecting specific targets for improvement, the group can identify criteria for monitoring progress and delineate steps to obtain and use feedback in ways that ensure further improvement.

By engaging in these activities, a board goes beyond merely demanding that others be held accountable; it demonstrates commitment to its own accountability as well. Board actions for modeling accountability are powerful examples to others inside and outside the organization, delivering the message that trustees take their public trust seriously and are committed to acting on the same principles they expect others to acknowledge. Such examples speak much louder than words.

Channeling Discontent

Another avenue by which attention to board performance may proceed builds directly upon trustee concerns or dissatisfactions with their board experiences, or suggestions for improvement. Concerns may be voiced as complaints about board meetings (for example, members' frustration that their time or skills are being misused, or that the wrong issues are taking up time and attention). Or, certain trustees may comment on incongruity between agenda items and time (or other resources) allotted to them. Other concerns may center on a particular individual who is blamed for a problem, or on whether the board needs new "stars."

It may be common for disgruntled trustees to complain during breaks or after a meeting closes, yet offer no constructive suggestion for improving the situation they complained about. Aside from allowing "vent time," covert exchanges do little toward elevating board performance. Some boards have so many change recommendations on the table that members cannot focus on key shared concerns in order to move forward together. None of these ways of voicing discontent is constructive to improvement dialogue.

However they are expressed, complaints or dissatisfactions are telling signals that trustees should take time to direct attention to its practices. Self-assessment questions should not be avoided but welcomed and addressed directly, because they are doorways to valuable changes. Every member should ponder whether he or she is doing as much as possible for the organization and if there are ways to do better. Then they should be prepared to discuss their concerns with the group and join in a mutual effort to find workable solutions.

If concerns are to advance into action for change, they must move from *individual judgment* to constructive *whole group attention*. Placing performance issues and change recommendations squarely on the table for thoughtful group scrutiny circumvents misunderstandings, clarifies resolve, and broadens group investment in altering practice patterns in ways that enhance board effectiveness.

It is essential to encourage dissatisfied trustees to engage in open dialogue so that other colleagues can join in diagnosing issues and searching for appropriate solutions. Rather than allowing blame and splits to fester ("us versus them"), leaders must keep individual member concerns accessible to group consideration. Conflicting views must be heard respectfully and attentively to arrive at consensus on issues diagnosis and prioritization. Only then will questions and concerns be owned by all, and the work of creating a stronger board become a mutual enterprise.

For example, complaints about length of board meetings or time-consuming digressions from agenda deliberations are cues for a board to step back and examine how well it is using its time and energy. Listed below are examples of productive questions that individual trustees have raised:

- Are we working on the most important issues facing this organization? How should we prioritize those issues and keep our attention focused on them?
- Should more explicit criteria guide how our agenda items are selected and ordered and how our meeting time is used?
- Are charges to our committees sufficiently explicit and clearly linked to our strategic priorities?
- Are questions put before us clear and specific, with major alternative responses set forth?
- Is background information presented to us in sufficient time to be digested and in appropriate form to be readily understood?
- Do all members share a common commitment to the board's expectations, responsibilities, and priorities?
- What appropriate steps can we take to improve these aspects of our work?

Conscientious work groups use members' assessments of meetings and procedures as a basis for launching discussions of possible improvement avenues. By bringing performance concerns into full group view, trustees can begin to build shared ownership of issues and mutual commitment to action. This crucial step allows them to come together around common concerns and develop more effective work patterns.

Building on difficult situations and celebrating successful ones afford opportunities for boards to learn and cultivate broader service capabilities. Skilled managers have long recognized the importance of identifying and rewarding successful performance while changing unsuccessful practices. Boards should adapt this outlook and take the time not only to celebrate successes, but to listen when stakeholders point out shortcomings. Time spent acknowledging a committee or task force for excellent work—perhaps doing so in meeting minutes, reports, and public announcements—further promotes effective work patterns.

Creating a Learning Organization: Leadership Roles

Board leaders, especially the chairperson and the CEO, play essential roles in the movement from individual concern to group responsibility. Often they are the first to hear members' concerns and, instead of avoiding them or defending the status quo, should invite their expressions of desire to improve board performance.

Old habits may suggest avoiding discontent, questions, or challenges to customary practice, but nonresponse can exacerbate divisiveness and create win–lose traps. Instead of repressing questions or allowing polarizations to develop, effective leaders solicit member assessments of meetings and bring concerns to the full group for its attention and response.

Not every complaint will meet with group consensus, but it may be easier for the complainer to take a different stance if all members listen and respond respectfully to the concern. Sometimes the initial issue or suggestion is reformulated by the group into a broader or more basic concern that all can join in addressing.

In most of the boards we examined, the earliest efforts to draw attention to performance and seek change originated with the executive. No longer content with cynical advice to "keep them in the dark so they'll leave you alone," savvy executives realize that their boards can be their best partners in creating stronger organizations. These executives invest extensive time in assessing group performance and educating members in order to maximize board contributions to the organization. This seems especially true when major changes loom; for example, whether to join a network, consider a merger, or plan for a capital campaign.

Whether prompted by their own concerns or comments from others, the CEO must be committed to improving board performance and take the initiative to bring such matters up with the full board. Working with the board chairperson, the executive raises performance questions before the group to see if others share the concerns. Together, they raise aspirations about what the board could be achieving and suggest alternative approaches. On issues where there is group interest and shared concern, leaders then help the group sharpen the focus of attention to those aspects members want to join in changing. The next step is to identify specific actions the group is ready to take. Throughout these processes, leaders raise group expectations and aspirations by initiating questions about group performance, suggesting alternative approaches to dealing with issues, and offering new possibilities for improving group effectiveness.

By opening up discussion about the board's performance, leaders show that it is appropriate to direct attention to the quality of the board's own work and to explore ways to improve it. Thus, they shift concerns from back channels to the forefront of everyone's attention to foster discussions of ways the group can better expedite its work in the future. Leaders provide opportunities for others to join in problem analysis and form a constituency for mutual action in seeking solutions.

Leaders serve a number of other vital functions during such discussions. Rather than avoiding discontent or treating it as an occasion for blame throwing or fault finding, they redirect questions into group responsibilities; model the behavior of respectful feedback; grasp the opportunity to improve performance quality; and invite others to join in similar efforts. In so doing, leaders confirm that they and the trustees are committed to doing their jobs more effectively, not just avoiding criticisms, blaming others, or settling for familiar ways and business as usual. This encourages dedication to improving the quality of group performance, even at the expense of traditional—and complacent—practices or assumptions.

Effective leaders expect and allow some anxiety over questioning old assumptions and giving up the familiar for the unknown. Their persistence in seeking improvements even when solutions may not yet be apparent encourages experimentation with new ways of dealing with tasks and invites members to try alternatives without fear of making mistakes. Leaders recognize and celebrate incremental steps toward goals of improved performance.

Visionary leaders apply Senge's (1994) advice about creating organizations that learn to work better as they move forward. Outstanding orchestras and winning sports teams exemplify groups that take time to reflect on each performance to assess how well they did and what changes might improve future efforts. Reflecting on experiences, identifying areas to change, and then implementing the changes are all crucial steps to their success. Boards that follow this model by examining and reflecting on their own performance can learn useful lessons and reveal changes that can turn them into more effective leaders who set the learning curve throughout their organization.

In conclusion, every organization encounters numerous situations that not only invite board reflection on its role and contributions in each situation, but also identify opportunities to lead more effectively. Successful conclusion of major projects, changes in external circumstances, leadership transitions, assumption reassessments, accountability issues, and trustee expressions of desire to do more for the organization all serve to extend discussion to viable steps the board might take to improve its own performance. In drawing on "milestone situations," effective boards examine and fine-tune their performance, which establishes them as models throughout their organization.

We next consider six sets of characteristics demonstrated by strong boards, showing how a trustee board can assess itself in those areas and describing practical steps for strengthening their governance systems.

Chapter 3

Building Instrumental Competencies

"What makes for effective trusteeship?" "Why are some boards more effective than others?" "Can our board become a high-performance team?" These questions should preoccupy all trustees, whether their organization is riding a wave of success or at risk of losing accreditation. Being deemed effective during one phase of an organization's life does not ensure that status at a later phase. However, trusteeship can be learned, strengthened, and transmitted from experienced members to newcomers; we can learn important lessons from boards that have excelled in their performance and maintained their level of effectiveness.

Recent studies of high-performance boards indicate that six distinctive skill sets characterize their performance (Chait, Holland, and Taylor, 1993). These skill sets, or dimensions of competency, include the following:

- *Strategic:* The board focuses most of its attention on issues and priorities that are vital to enhancing the organization's future.
- *Contextual:* The board's decision making is guided by a clear, shared understanding of the organization's mission, culture, and values.
- *Analytical:* The board examines all sides of issues and engages effectively in problem solving.
- *Political:* The board takes the necessary steps to build and maintain good relationships with all organization stakeholders.
- *Educational:* The board is well informed about the organization and about trustee roles and responsibilities.
- *Interpersonal:* The board functions well as a cohesive group and manages conflict appropriately.

These dimensions fall into two broad skill clusters: those that are instrumental or task oriented, and those that are social or relational in nature. *Instrumental competencies* encompass the strategic, contextual, and analytical dimensions. *Social competencies* include the political, educational, and interpersonal areas. No single member need excel in all six areas, but as a cohesive work group effective boards intentionally cultivate each area.

In this chapter, we examine the first three skill sets, define how a board can assess its performance in each one, and describe practices used by effective health care organization boards in exercising these skills. In chapter 4, we address the three social competencies and discuss ways to assess and develop them.

The Strategic Dimension

Effective boards are strategically competent. They keep a sharp eye on the future, identify trends in the political and social environment, and formulate responses that position their organization for future success. Their active involvement in envisioning and shaping institutional direction ensures a strategic approach to the organization's future position. Such boards cultivate and concentrate on processes that sharpen priorities and direct attention to a few key matters of symbolic magnitude to the organization. In effect, strategically attuned boards anticipate problems, acting before issues become urgent rather than merely putting out today's fires.

Strategic competency enables board members to see how today's decisions move the organization toward desired future status. Exercising this skill requires that the group learn about emerging trends and changes in public policy, technology, and community needs. The board uses this information to identify priorities, formulate goals, and set directions for the future. These choices provide the framework for program development or changes, policies and guidelines for implementation, and plans for deploying financial and human resources.

Strategic planning skills enable a board to link its conclusions about the future with its understanding of the present organizational capacities and needs. Opportunities and threats in the external environment must be examined along with strengths and weaknesses within the organization. Balancing such factors and setting clear priorities in the context of organization mission are key strategic planning steps. The conclusions of these efforts provide the organization with a sense of purpose and direction and guide its use of human and financial resources.

The strategic planning process begins with a comprehensive assessment of anticipated trends, with special attention given to emerging issues and projected changes in the external environment. Trustees should examine key directions in specific areas, such as:

- Public policy
- Social and community needs

- Expected changes in health care technology and labor force resources
- Trends in the business environment and among competitors

Many useful resources for carrying out such an assessment are readily available from national health care associations, such as the American Hospital Association.

While expediting a trends assessment, the board should also work closely with management to conduct rigorous internal organizational analyses that identify strengths and limitations in areas such as those listed below:

- Training and staff reputation
- Indicators of service quality
- Management structures
- State of technical resources
- Match between services offered and patient needs
- Consumer satisfaction
- Service gaps and unmet needs

All performance indicators in these crucial areas should be identified and monitored regularly by the board.

These two analysis streams—external environmental trends and internal strengths and limitations—should yield a picture of areas where the organization might consolidate its strengths and areas in which it might expand or specialize to respond to opportunities for better performance. Analyses also may identify organizational aspects requiring change, or activities that could be eliminated so as to redeploy resources. Choices in these areas position the organization for success in the coming years. More specifically, they guide board efforts to chart the organization's course as well as staff efforts to implement policy decisions.

Many boards focus attention on day-to-day operations and neglect longer-term perspectives. Member concerns for improving the quality of existing services and increasing patient satisfaction can become ends in themselves rather than means, a strategy that can ensure more effective organizational performance in the future. In this context, then, quality improvement efforts (such as reengineering) may not sufficiently address essential questions like "What business should this organization be in?" and "What services should it carry out with optimal quality?" Therefore, questions about facility renovations, for example, can be addressed in terms of costs and feasibility of alternative approaches, *or* they can be grounded in the essential question of how the activity envisioned in this site fits into the *overall future plan for the whole institution.* In all deliberations, it is imperative that the board remain focused on the future, rather than fixed only on today's operational details.

One consequence of neglecting strategic planning and analysis may be seen in the experiences of hospitals that rushed into chemical dependency treatment programs. Rather than carefully examining how drug abuse or alcoholism treatment programs fit with their organization's mission and values, certain boards and CEOs saw an opportunity to fill empty beds. Instead of carefully examining community needs, resources, and trends, their short-range focus honed in on a new reimbursement stream, leading to the conversion of unused beds (many of them maternity beds) into chemical dependency beds. Unfortunately, they found themselves unprepared for the level of service demands; choruses of disappointment arose when they had to back out of these programs. The moral? Effective strategic planning on the front end can help circumvent future disaster.

Another application of strategic competence is embodied in board member complaints that "there just isn't time to get to the important issues." This signals a need for the board to reassess how it uses a precious and scarce resource—its own time and energy. Routine items and lengthy committee reports at the top of the agenda, for example, consume time that could be spent more wisely on targeted questions about the organization's future.

When difficult but important questions fall at the end of a meeting, when energy is low and attention is shifting toward their next appointment, trustees risk addressing key issues only in a superficial manner. Planning meeting agendas more thoughtfully can result in concentrated attention to crucial organizational matters.

The number and length of formal board meetings may be specified in the bylaws and board rules. It is not unusual for these documents also to outline the order of meeting business. Changing constrictive rules is one step toward freeing a board's energy and creativity. Even without such rule changes, there are many ways to modify meetings to allow time for work on important issues. The consent agenda is one such strategic technique.

In planning the meeting agenda, officers can divide issues into two groups: one composed of routine items that require attention but do not warrant extensive discussion; the other made up of a few key matters requiring fuller discussion and analysis. Routine items (such as approval of the previous meeting's minutes, announcements of future events, dissemination of committee reports, and the like) can be clustered into a *consent agenda* for a single vote. This dispenses with material that otherwise would have invited tangential, time-consuming discussions.

Any member can request that an item be taken off the consent agenda and put on the floor for discussion; most members welcome the additional time for work on the more important matters. Consent agendas succeed only if all members agree to the plan and all are conscientious about reading background material disseminated prior to the meeting. Consent agendas are counterproductive, however, if members distrust one another or read the material only during the meeting.

Another technique for helping trustees assess their performance in strategic competency is taken from descriptions of the behaviors of high-performance boards (Holland, 1991). After each person rates the board, ask where the board could improve and what work aspects provide possible avenues for improvement. Then compare ratings and improvement ideas to see where shared concerns meet. Often, differences in perceptions of a board come from members seeing aspects of it that others may have missed. Exploring these views can enrich understanding of the board and yield creative improvement ideas.

When assessing board performance in this dimension, begin with the broad question "How well does this board help envision and shape organizational direction and ensure a strategic approach to its future?" Next examine how accurately each of the following statements describes your experience with this board:

1. I have attended board meetings where discussion focused on identifying or overcoming specific weaknesses in the organization.
2. This board is more involved in preparing for the future than in trying to put out today's fires.
3. This board does not delay action until an issue becomes urgent or critical.
4. This board has not evaded responsibility for an important issue facing the organization.
5. Within the past year, this board has reviewed organization strategies for attaining its long-term goals.
6. The board discusses events and trends in the larger environment that may present specific opportunities for the organization.
7. The board sets clear priorities for the organization to pursue in the coming year.
8. The board makes explicit use of the long-range organization priorities in dealing with current issues.
9. Our board meetings tend to focus more on preparing for the future than on current concerns.
10. This board often discusses where the organization should be in five or more years hence.
11. More than half of board time is spent discussing issues of importance to the organization's long-range future.
12. At least once a year, the board asks the executive to articulate a vision for the organization's future and strategies for realizing that vision.

In computing your board's score, allow a point for each item you agree with. A total score of 10–12 indicates considerable strength in this competency; 7–9 indicates a mixed picture—some strengths and some weaknesses; 6 or lower suggests that the board needs to give extensive attention to improving performance in this area.

Next it is useful for trustees to compare their answers and identify alternative views of board performance and possible reasons. Discussing different views can result in valuable insights into a group's level of function. Members who give lower performance ratings may recognize problems undetected by other members; conversely, higher ratings may indicate performance strengths overlooked by others. By discussing differences in perception, trustees can arrive at new insights about board performance and identify aspects on which there is shared concern for change.

The next step is to determine, as a group, what steps the board might take to improve its strategic competency. Listed here are some ways in which high-performance boards have worked to strengthen their skill in this area:

- Request that the CEO develop an annual Memorandum of Strategy for board review.
- Establish priorities, a detailed annual work plan, and meeting agenda schedule for the board and its committees, based on the CEO's memorandum.
- Structure board meetings to concentrate on strategic priorities.
- Prioritize agenda items, listing the most important issues first.
- Invite the CEO to provide an overview of major topics and the linkages among committees' charges.
- Ask the appropriate senior staff officer to provide (prior to meetings) a brief preface to each major policy issue so as to place the issue in a larger context.
- Ask appropriate senior officers to provide (prior to meetings) key questions for the board to discuss.
- Display prominently the board's priorities and its annual work plan.
- Reserve time at each meeting to discuss whatever is uppermost in the executive's mind.
- Operate with a consent agenda.
- Develop an information system to keep the board abreast of movement toward its priorities.
- Monitor how the board spends its time.
- Be sure clinical staff leaders serve on appropriate board committees.

Not all of these practices may be appropriate for your board. They are offered as suggestions; discussing them can lead to identifying other ways to strengthen board strategic competency.

The Contextual Dimension

Trustees with strong contextual competency are conversant with issues facing the health care organization and the larger society. They understand and take into account the culture and norms of the organization they govern. They intentionally rely on the organization's mission, values, and traditions to guide their decisions. Through trustee actions, the board exemplifies and reinforces its core values.

Today's actions must be grounded in organization values, traditions, and mission *and* be aligned with external environmental changes. Trustees who fail to grasp the implications either of the mission and purpose or of external changes can compromise not only board decisions but organizational effectiveness.

Changes in public policies, technology, and competitor programs are pushing provider organizations to adapt quickly in order to survive. Such adaptation may steer an organization into new markets or service areas, forcing leaders to question whether these new directions are congruent with the organization's original mission. Effective boards address linkage between markets and mission, building on organizational traditions and values and adapting them to underway environmental changes.

For example, current public policies and insurance regulations call for fewer inpatient days, which leads to more acutely ill patients at admission. This results from increased emphasis on outpatient and ambulatory care, incentives to reduce hospitalization rates, and better home care. These alternative health care approaches may be consistent with the organization's basic mission, but they jeopardize financial resources, for they require changes in service patterns as well as revenue sources. Finding ways to draw on the organization's mission and values while ensuring survival is a complex board challenge that demands hard work and creative thinking.

Trustees can use the following exercise to assess their performance in contextual competency. Similar to the strategic competency skill set, the exercise is taken from descriptions of high-performance boards (Chait, Holland, and Taylor, 1993). After each person rates the board, members should compare conclusions and then discuss where their board might improve and which aspects suggest avenues for improvement. Compare ratings and improvement ideas to see where members share concerns.

Begin by asking the broad question "To what extent are our decisions guided by a clear, shared understanding of the organization's mission, culture, and values?" Then examine how accurately each of the following statements describes your experience on this board:

1. New trustee orientation programs include a segment about the organization's history and traditions.

2. In discussing key issues, it is not unusual for someone on the board to talk about "what this organization stands for" and how that is related to the matter at hand.
3. Values are often discussed explicitly at board meetings.
4. This board has not made a key decision that I believe to be inconsistent with organization mission.
5. I have been present in board meetings where discussions of the organization's history and mission were key factors in resolving a problem.
6. It is apparent from trustees' comments that they understand the organization's mission very well.
7. The board's own actions are consistent with the organization's deepest values.
8. Upon joining the board, new members are provided a detailed explanation of the organization's mission.
9. The board reviews the organization's mission at least once every five years.
10. One reason I joined this board was a strong belief in the organization's values.
11. Our decision making is guided by a clear understanding of our mission, culture, and values.
12. Former board members have participated in special events designed to convey to new members the organization's history and values.
13. The board understands the norms of professions within this organization.

In computing your board's score, add a point for each item you agree with. Again, a score of 10 or more indicates considerable strength in this aspect of performance; 7–9 indicates a mix of strengths and limitations; 6 or lower suggests that this board needs to give careful attention to making improvements in this area. It is useful for members to compare their responses and discuss differing perceptions of the board's performance.

Next, consider steps the board might take to improve its skill in contextual competency. Listed here are some ways in which high-performance boards have sought to strengthen their competency in this area:

- Include in orientations an explicit introduction to organizational values, norms, and traditions.
- Invite retired staff, board members, administrators, and "living legends" to relate the organization's history.
- Invite current staff leaders to discuss concepts of shared governance, collegiality, and consensus.

- Review the organization's hallmark characteristics and bedrock values that set it apart from competitors.
- Resocialize trustees to the board's role and the organization's values through a brief reading, pledge, or anecdote.
- Be aware of actions and decisions as statements of value.
- Attend a joint luncheon or meeting with trustees from another facility.

As noted before, not all of these practices may be right for your board. They are suggestions for consideration. Your discussions of the topic may lead to ideas that work better to improve board performance in this area.

The Analytical Dimension

The analytical dimension of board performance focuses on group skill in examining the complex issues the board faces. Effective boards recognize complexities and subtleties in issues before the organization and draw on multiple perspectives when dissecting problems and identifying appropriate responses. Because they recognize that important issues in governance involve ambiguities that rarely yield to perfect solutions, they search widely for relevant information and draw on multiple viewpoints from various constituencies.

No decision is made in a vacuum. All board actions are interrelated—decisions on one issue influence the manner in which the group approaches other issues. To understand underlying linkages across matters before them, effective boards draw on analytical and critical skills to identify "subissues" and address them directly. Techniques may include one or more of the following: brainstorming, questioning group assumptions and habits, examining alternative approaches to problem solving, exploring possible implications of proposed actions, viewing options from the perspectives of various constituencies, and considering the advantages and disadvantages of each alternative.

Possessing analytical skill does not mean that every trustee is an expert in every issue facing the organization. Nor does it mean that every trustee must be conversant on current tax law, hazardous waste disposal regulations, occupational safety, or other intricate topics. However, the board *is* responsible for ensuring that their deliberations draw on the knowledge of experts in the field relevant to the issue being discussed; this way, members understand the choices before them and the implications of alternative directions. Also, the board exercises strong, critical thinking while examining choices and reaching conclusions.

A key resource for analytical competency lies in the composition of the board itself. Diversity among trustees facilitates bringing multiple viewpoints to bear on issues before the board. For example, older (50s–70s), white males traditionally have dominated most hospital boards, whereas service recipients have been far more demographically diverse. Board composition should reflect the whole community being served and include individuals who will represent all constituent interests, as well as communicate board concerns and actions back to the service community. To accomplish this objective, trustees should seek balance of age, ethnicity, gender, and interests as reflected throughout the organization. Doing so ensures diversity of views, concerns, and skills, which in turn enriches the quality of analysis. Otherwise, a self-perpetuating board will merely clone itself.

Boards should cultivate members' analytical skills. Otherwise, they risk passive acceptance of custom and habit in deliberations (automatically deferring to committee and management recommendations, for example). Members should be encouraged to raise critical questions about proposed solutions, challenge assumptions, brainstorm about alternative approaches to resolving problems, seek creative direction—in general, try innovative ways of addressing issues.

Complacent boards tend to discourage challenges to administration recommendations. These boards allow blind spots to limit their creativity. Only rigorous critical analysis of issues and recommendations can pave the way for more creative solutions that will better serve the organization.

In examining your board's practices in this area, begin with the broad questions "To what extent does this board recognize complexities and subtleties in the issues it faces?" "Does this board draw on multiple perspectives to dissect complex problems and synthesize appropriate responses?" Then examine how accurately each of the following statements reflects your board's behavior:

1. The board takes regular steps to stay informed about significant trends in the larger environment that might affect the organization.
2. I have attended board meetings where it was evident that subtleties surrounding issues we dealt with were well understood by all members.
3. Our board explicitly examines the downside or possible pitfalls of an important decision under review.
4. Many issues our board deals with seem to be interrelated.
5. Our decisions on one issue tend to influence what we do about other issues that come before us.
6. We are clear about the key issues this board faces.
7. When faced with an important issue, the board often brainstorms to generate a list of creative approaches or solutions to a problem.
8. When issues come before our board, they are framed in such way that members see the connections between matters at hand and the organization's overall strategy.

9. When dealing with a complex matter, the board often requests that a decision be postponed until further information can be obtained.
10. Administration's recommendations are subjected to careful questioning during board meetings.
11. The board does not avoid ambiguous and complicated issues.
12. The board takes on policy questions that do not have clear answers.
13. Our board seeks information and advice from leaders of other similar organizations.

To compute your board's score, add a point for each item you agree with. A total score of 10 or more indicates considerable strength in this competency; 7–9 indicates a mixed picture (some strengths, some weaknesses); 6 or lower suggests a need for extensive attention to improving your board's analytical competency. Compare ratings among members and discuss possible reasons for differing perceptions. Are there aspects of this competency that members want to work on as a team?

Next, identify ways to strengthen analytical skills. Some of the tactics that high-performance boards use to develop analytical skills are listed below (not all may be suited to your organization):

- Foster "cognitive complexity" by using multiple viewpoints to analyze issues and events.
- Seek concrete, even contradictory, information on ambiguous matters.
- Ask a few members to serve as critical evaluators or devil's advocates by pointing out disadvantages of recommendations and worst case scenarios.
- Develop contingency plans.
- Ask members to assume the perspective of key constituencies by role playing.
- Brainstorm, silently or openly.
- Establish goals for revenues, expenses, investments, capital expenditures, and other financial items.
- Consult outsiders and persons serving on other boards.
- Use group techniques such as nominal group or delphi exercises (in which each member offers a suggestion or possible solution before evaluating any of them) to elicit all members' views and decision by consensus on a given issue.
- Reinforce and reward constructive criticism.
- Make sure each trustee/director reads the auditor's "management letter" from the most recent financial statement.
- Learn about the changing roles of health professionals – physicians, nurses, occupational therapists, social workers, and others.

- Urge committees to give rationale for their recommendations *and* for options not selected.

In conclusion, strategic, contextual, and analytical skills are vital for effective governance. Any group can examine its own performance in these areas and adapt some of the steps others have taken to strengthen board effectiveness. In chapter 4, we take up three additional competencies that are more social or relational in their emphasis.

Chapter 4

Building Social Competencies

Effective boards complement instrumental skills with competencies that are more social or relational in nature—the political, educational, and interpersonal dimensions. Many trustees are more comfortable addressing the instrumental skills than they are in discussing the relational ones mainly because they value accomplishment of tasks over comfortable relationships. Nevertheless, relational skills are vital for effective teamwork, because they allow a group to evaluate how well it exercises responsibilities for clear communication, whether its learning is experiential, and how it rates in terms of building team cohesion. In this chapter, we review these areas, showing how a board can self-assess performance in each dimension. We also describe some ways effective health care organization boards practice relational competencies.

The Political Dimension

A primary board responsibility is to develop and sustain healthy relationships and maintain open, two-way communication with all constituencies—staff, patients, sponsors, donors, suppliers, and the community—all of whom have a stake in its success. Trustees must respect the integrity of the governance process, and the legitimate roles and interests of stakeholders. When dealing with issues that may affect constituents, they must communicate with them regularly and directly, being certain that their interests are conveyed accurately. Board members should seek problem resolution and decision making without polarization among constituencies, or without win–lose outcomes. Finally, they should cultivate alliances with other community organizations and health care providers.

All of these imperatives rely on political skills, which are essential to effective governance. They enable a board to understand and balance multiple interests of diverse constituencies while arriving at solutions that sustain organizational goodwill toward all stakeholders. Differing or conflicting interests are inevitable, but to remain unaware of, or insensitive to, varied interests can lead a board to decisions that exacerbate friction and dilute loyalty to the organization. Because board actions affect so many people, clearly delineated processes for open, two-way communication with all interest groups are essential to political competency.

In addition to communication channels with internal staff, suppliers, insurers, donors, and sponsors, the board must ensure open access with the external community, whose leaders may have their own perceptions of the hospital, its actions, and its problems. Understanding public perceptions, then, is vital to reaching decisions that enable the organization to serve its community and sustain its trust.

In examining your board's political performance, begin with two questions: "To what extent does this board accept as one of its primary responsibilities the need to develop and maintain healthy relationships among key constituencies?" "How well does it carry out these responsibilities?" Then rate how accurately each of the following statements describes your board:

1. Our board has had or formed ad hoc committees or task forces co-chaired by or composed of a staff member(s) and a board member(s).
2. An annual report on board activities is prepared and distributed publicly.
3. The board communicates its decisions to everyone affected by them.
4. If our board thinks a key constituent group will disagree with a pending action, we investigate their feelings before making a final decision.
5. Specific board members are responsible for maintaining communication channels with specific key community leaders.
6. This board gives as much attention to *how* it reaches conclusions as it does to *what* is being decided.
7. I have attended meetings where explicit attention was given to concerns of the community or a population served by the organization.
8. The board periodically requests and considers information on morale among the organization's professional staff.
9. Before reaching a decision on important issues, the board usually requests input from persons and groups likely to be affected by that decision.
10. The board is keenly aware of what impact its decisions will have within our service community.
11. The administration regularly reports to the board concerns from the organization's service population.

In computing your board's score, add a point for each statement you agree with. A total score of 9 or more indicates considerable strength in this political competency; 6–8 indicates a mixed picture of strengths and weaknesses; 5 or lower suggests that the board needs to give extensive attention to improving its performance in this area. Compare ratings among board members and discuss possible reasons for differences in views.

Next, identify possible ways to strengthen the board's political skills performance. Suggestions drawn from the practices of high-performance boards are offered below:

- Distribute annually a profile of board members.
- Distribute publicly an annual board report and board agenda.
- Appoint staff and consumers to serve on board committees.
- Invite staff to address the board periodically.
- Monitor relationships and morale within the organization.
- Keep options open and avoid win–lose situations.
- Remain sensitive to the legitimate roles and responsibilities of stakeholders and to the integrity of the governance process.
- Visit staff on their own turf—a "grand rounds" for trustees.
- Establish multiconstituency task forces.

Your discussions of possible approaches to this area may identify more appropriate directions for your board.

The Educational Dimension

Effective boards ensure that all trustees are well informed about their organization; the professions represented within it; the board's role(s), responsibilities, and performance expectations; and health care trends and changes. Toward this end they carve out opportunities for trustees' education and development; seek feedback on their performance; reflect periodically on their work; assess their strengths and limitations; and examine mistakes or missed opportunities. In short, effective boards are intentional learners.

"Learning organizations" have become widely recognized as environments vital to survival in a world of rapid change (Senge, 1990). Taking time to learn from the group experience and to identify areas for improvement are essential to effective team development. Given the stringent demands on board members' time, trustees must endorse learning climates if their board and organization are to thrive.

Both internal and external environmental changes affect the learning process. *Internally,* board membership changes over time, and newcomers should learn as much as possible about the organization, how trends in the external environment affect it, and how the board operates. *Externally*, global shifts (in information technology, and labor and population trends, for example) affect how provider organizations deliver health care. Understanding the implications of change in both environments is essential to effective governance.

Board seminars and workshops can keep trustees up-to-date on these crucial areas. Public officials, health care associations, and medical societies (on state and local levels) are credible resources for board presentations. An education task force can survey trustees to identify issues or topics they would like to learn more about, work with the administration to identify appropriate speakers, and then schedule times for educational sessions.

High-performance boards go even further by actively seeking performance feedback from one another, from senior staff, and from outside observers. They take advantage of this information to identify aspects of their work that need strengthening; reflect on past decisions that proved to be inappropriate (ill-informed or ill-timed); and use feedback on their efforts to fine-tune decisions and adjust their course of action.

In chapter 5, we discuss several approaches to performing board assessments. An example, however, is offered for purposes of our discussion here. A board might begin self-assessment in educational competency by inviting brief feedback from participants at the conclusion of meetings. It can expand these comments into more systematic evaluations from additional sources. Results can be examined at an annual retreat that focuses on strengths and limitations in the past year and sets improvement goals for the coming year.

Examining your board's educational skills also can begin with a broad question: "To what extent does our board take steps to ensure that members are well informed about the organization, the professions within it, and the board's roles, responsibilities, and performance?" Then assess how well each of the following statements describes your board experience:

1. I have participated in board discussions about what we should do differently as a result of a mistake the board made or an opportunity it missed.
2. At least once every two years, our board holds a retreat or special session to examine our performance.
3. The board periodically sets aside time to learn more about important issues facing organizations similar to the one we govern.
4. I can recall an occasion when the board acknowledged its responsibility for an ill-advised or ill-timed decision.
5. Most of our trustees do not depend only on observation and informal discussions to learn about their role and duties.
6. We make sure that someone serves as mentor to help newcomers learn the ropes.

7. I have participated in board discussions about how effective our performance is.
8. I have participated in discussions with new members about trustee roles and responsibilities.
9. I have participated in board discussions about what we can learn from a mistake we made.
10. I have received clear feedback on my performance as a board member.
11. The board allocates organization funds for member education and development.
12. Our board has conducted an explicit examination of its roles and responsibilities.

In calculating your board's score, add a point for each statement you agree with. A total score of 10 or more indicates strong board performance in this area; 7–9 suggests a mixed picture of strengths and limitations; 6 or lower suggests that the board should give extensive consideration to making improvements in this area. Next, compare your answers with other trustees to identify areas where there is shared concern and interest in improvement. Then consider some of the ways that other boards have sought to strengthen their educational skills; see if some are adaptable to your board.

- Set aside time at each board meeting for a miniseminar to learn about an important matter or process, or to discuss a selected reading.
- Conduct 24- to 48-hour retreats every year or two for the same purpose and analyze feedback on board performance.
- Ask board members and senior staff to briefly report on the best idea they heard at a recent conference or meeting.
- Meet periodically with "role counterparts" from boards of comparable organizations.
- Rotate committee assignments.
- Review and compare compensation ratios and indicators of organizational performance in the local health care service area.
- Have an annual "pop quiz" about the board and its organization.
- Establish internal feedback mechanisms by requesting comments at the end of each meeting, either by going once around the room or submitting suggestions on an index card.
- Invite comments on board performance from senior staff through a third party.
- Review patient feedback results periodically.
- Discuss selected critical incidents at a retreat.
- Conduct an annual survey of board members on their individual performance and the board's collective performance.

- Expand the role of the Nominating Committee to include monitoring the board's performance and overall health.
- Invite an outsider to observe board meetings and provide feedback.
- Invite regional and national industry representatives to address the board about opportunities and pressures facing health care organizations.

The Interpersonal Dimension

Boards should nurture development of members *as a group*, beyond the occasional assembly of talented individuals. Attention should focus specifically on the board's collective well-being and foster a sense of collegiality and cohesiveness among all participants. Interpersonal skills development enables the board to draw effectively on the talents of every member and to create a team where the whole is more than simply the sum of its parts.

The board–CEO relationship, critical to organizational success, is a linkage that is vital to effective teamwork and therefore must be cultivated conscientiously. Some CEOs, fearing that a strong board will diminish their power, avoid initiatives to strengthen the board. This win–lose approach leads to tension and underperformance of executive and board alike. Although board involvement in operational matters is inappropriate, its involvement in synthesizing divergent views into coherent policies and identifying creative alternatives for future growth are critical factors for organization success.

Some members complain that the CEO does not provide appropriate information in a timely manner that facilitates thoughtful board analysis. Consequently, they feel ill-informed, unprepared to deal with issues, and condemned to operational trivia. On the other hand, some CEOs complain that their boards waste time on minor issues, pass inconsistent or useless policies, avoid conflict of interest issues, and neglect attending to their own performance. These patterns can be changed through purposeful efforts. The board should identify what it considers relevant governance information (as distinct from management information) and focus on indicators such as changes in patient satisfaction, budget exceptions, or trends in utilization rates.

A number of boards have struggled with the dilemma of whether to make the CEO a voting member of the board. Debate has been extensive, and we have seen strong boards on both sides of the issue. A recent report by the Independent Sector (a national association of nonprofit organizations) noted that nonprofit boards are split 50/50 on the matter of full board membership for the CEO. Many CEOs sit on the board in an *ex officio* capacity, upon termination of their job tenure. This allows the individual to continue as an integral part of the team.

However, potential conflicts of interest can arise for the CEO who is a full member of the board, given that that body is responsible for recruitment, retention, oversight, and termination of the CEO. Likewise, a voting CEO risks conflict of interest when issues of compensation and performance appraisal arise. Similar problems may surface in dealing with questions of downsizing, reorganization, or investment decisions.

We recommend that the CEO be an active participant in issues before the board, but only those that do not create a conflict of interest. This is a full portfolio and does not need to be complicated by concerns of voting or recusing oneself from decisions. Each board must find the practice that fits with its history, values, and goals.

A more fundamental concern is the nature of the board–CEO interaction. Once having hired this person, many boards revert to a passive role, relying on executive initiative in all matters and then watching for mistakes.

Successful boards take the reins in ensuring that they identify the most important issues facing the organization and obtain the most relevant information to monitor movement on those issues. They cultivate a strong sense of partnership with the executive and with one another, instead of acting only as watchdogs. Rather than assuming that the executive carries all burdens of responsibility for the organization's success, they see themselves as partners in guiding the ship and fine-tuning the course as events unfold. All members share responsibility for concentrating on the most crucial issues facing the organization in the coming years.

To nurture such partnerships, strong boards take time for members to become well acquainted with one another, both professionally and personally. Social events (dinners and trips) and recognition of individual accomplishments (boardroom or media announcements) are important activities toward this end. Interactions outside the boardroom round out members' acquaintances with one another as valuable team members, not just placeholders around the boardroom table. Savvy boards foster inclusiveness, making certain that no one is left out of the loop or ignored during deliberations. Expenditures for such events must be reasonably related to the tax-exempt purposes of the organization.

Effective governing boards also direct explicit attention to developing leadership skills among members and ensuring that specific individuals are prepared to assume officer roles in the future. They make sure that expectations of membership are clearly understood by everyone, and they rely on feedback, professional development plans, or growth contracts (see chapter 5) to nurture leadership skills. Strong boards apply term limitations to provide graceful exits for underperformers or those whose contributions have ended.

Periodic self-assessment provides opportunities for members to decide whether they wish to continue their board service, what steps they want to take in order to strengthen their contributions, and what suggestions they offer for overall board improvement. The Committee on Nominations and Board Development can oversee such assessments and apply findings to planning educational sessions (as well as farewell dinners). It can also identify skills to look for in nominees to the board.

Begin assessing your board's performance in this area with the broad question "How well does this board nurture development of its members as a group, attend to the board's collective welfare, and foster a sense of cohesiveness?" Then examine how well each of the following statements describes your board experience:

1. I have had conversations with other members of the board regarding common interests we share outside our organization.
2. Differences of opinion in board decisions are settled more often through further discussion than by vote.
3. I have disagreed openly with other members in board meetings.
4. At our board meetings, there is at least as much dialogue _among_ members as there is between members and administrators.
5. Our board leadership typically goes out of its way to make sure that all members have the same information on important issues.
6. The board has adopted explicit goals for itself, distinct from goals it set for the total organization.
7. The board cultivates future board leaders, rather than relying only on natural emergence of leadership.
8. Seldom do other board members have important information that I lack on key issues.
9. I am able to speak my mind on key issues without fear of being ostracized by other trustees.
10. The board recognizes special events in the lives of its members.
11. Our board provides biographical information that helps members get to know one another better.
12. Members attend most of the social events sponsored by our organization.

In calculating your board's score, add a point for each statement you agree with. A total score of 10 or more indicates considerable strength in this competency; 7-9 indicates a mixed picture of strengths and weaknesses; 6 or lower suggests that the board needs to give extensive attention to improving its interpersonal skill performance.

Next, compare your answers with other board members, discussing reasons for differing perceptions. Then identify aspects of the board's interpersonal relationships on which there is shared concern and interest in change. You may be able to adapt some of the following steps other boards have used to strengthen their performance in this area:

- Organize events that enable board members to become better acquainted with one another socially and personally.
- Produce annually a notebook with up-to-date biographical sketches of each member.
- Build some "slack time" into the schedule for informal interaction.
- Share information widely and communicate regularly with every member.
- Be sure that everyone understands the unwritten, tacit "rules of the game."
- Have trustees sign a formal conflict of interest statement annually.
- Pair each newcomer with a mentor or coach.
- Establish and publicize annual goals for the board.
- Systematically groom the board's future leaders.
- Develop a "farm system" for identifying, recruiting, and cultivating new trustees.
- Use member growth contracts or professional development plans to improve individual performance.
- Be sure each trustee understands the board's bylaws, and rules and regulations.
- Develop an open, comprehensive CEO performance appraisal system.
- Link performance appraisal to goal setting.

In conclusion, questions for assessing performance in each of the six competency dimensions described here and in chapter 3 allow a board to self-examine and identify aspects members want to work on together for improvement. We turn now to other procedures and tools for assessing performance and identifying specific areas that may need attention.

Chapter 5

Assessing Performance and Identifying Targets for Change

Moving concerns about the board from an *individual plane* to *shared commitments and group action* can be propelled by systematic assessment or evaluation of board strengths and weaknesses. Many boards have made productive use of an array of assessment tools to identify performance components they want to work on together. These tools include group and individual self-assessment forms, constituency surveys, and outside expert reviews. Trustees should experiment with several approaches and identify the most useful and informative ones that meet their unique needs. We begin with some simple tools and proceed to more extensive ones.

End-of-Meeting Feedback

The easiest way to begin assessment is by taking a few minutes at the end of each meeting to solicit participants' views of how well the work went and what they might do to improve the next meeting. It is important to consider both areas—what *was* done and what *could be* done. Leaders can invite attention to various aspects of the board's work. For example:

- Relative importance of agenda items
- Clarity of linkage between agenda items and strategic priorities
- Relevance and helpfulness of materials or resources presented
- Specificity of questions before the group
- Adequacy of opportunities for individual members' input
- Overuse or underuse of "air time" by individual participants
- Clarity of conclusions
- Feasibility of next steps
- Meeting structure or processes
- Leadership roles
- Recommendations for subsequent sessions

Leaders then can summarize key points and apply them in planning and carrying out the next meeting.

For groups whose members may be reluctant to voice concerns or criticisms openly, comments or suggestions can be written anonymously on 3" × 5" index cards or note paper. Questions ("How appropriate was each agenda item for this group?" "Were thoughtful and realistic alternatives presented and examined?") may be designed to be as general or specific as necessary.

Once all feedback is collected, leaders identify major themes or patterns, report conclusions at the next meeting, then factor them into subsequent meetings. Alternatively, a task group might be chartered to collect, summarize, and report assessment findings back to the larger group. This should minimize leader or member bias.

This approach to self-assessment is easily introduced, nonthreatening, and productive of valuable feedback. Other benefits are that participants get to express concerns and suggestions while they are fresh in mind, and leaders learn what changes might increase meeting productivity as well as participants' satisfaction. Ultimately, everyone benefits from a sense of group ownership and responsibility for the quality of meetings—all with only a few minutes' time investment. Positive outcomes from evaluating meetings have encouraged many boards to proceed with more extensive and systematic evaluation methods. An example of one board's meeting evaluation form is shown in figure 5-1.

Formal Self-Evaluation Tools

A more extensive assessment approach builds upon member evaluations to create formal questionnaires that systematically address a wide range of board responsibilities. For each area of responsibility, an assessment scale rates answers to questions about specific aspects of board work. These questions invite respondents to judge each aspect along a spectrum (from "excellent" to "needs improvement"; or "strong," "moderate," and "weak"). Some instruments also include open-ended questions for trustee comments ("How can we improve our performance in this area?") These tools allow a board to evaluate its performance systematically in a number of important areas and draw conclusions about specific issues or work components that may need attention.

The Joint Commission on Accreditation of Healthcare Organizations (JCAHO) publishes standards for governance boards, with scoring instructions for each standard. JCAHO standards address the following performance dimensions:

- Documentation of board governance responsibilities and structures
- Explicit governance functions in areas including patient care, performance improvement, risk management, credentialing, and financial management

Figure 5-1.   Board Meeting Evaluation Form

Please rate each agenda item on each criterion, using high/medium/low or other scale.

Criteria	Agenda Item 1	Agenda Item 2	Agenda Item 3	Agenda Item 4	Agenda Item 5	Agenda Item 6
Appropriateness for board?						
Adequate background information?						
Issue focused on strategic priority?						
Question for board made clear?						
Alternatives presented and examined?						
Discussion focused?						
Appropriate time spent on issue?						
Specific decision reached?						
Implementation steps specified?						
Adequate resources allocated?						

Suggestions for improving future meetings:

- How bylaws address organizational purposes, legal accountabilities, responsibilities to patient population served, membership selection, and conflicts of interest
- Provisions for medical staff participation in governance
- Criteria and procedures for selection of the chief executive officer
- Compliance with applicable laws and regulations
- Processes for developing, reviewing, and revising policies
- System for conflict resolution

Health care organization boards should be familiar with these standards and use them judiciously in periodic performance self-assessments. Identified weak areas should be addressed in an improvement plan.

An excellent tool for self-assessment by hospital boards has been developed by The Governance Institute (Pointer and Ewell, 1994). This questionnaire, designed specifically to address JCAHO requirements, includes forms for hospital boards and for system boards. Each one guides the respondent through sets of questions about how board work is perceived in certain areas:

- Mission and planning
- Quality of staff
- Financial health of the organization
- Support and evaluation of management
- Effectiveness of the board's own performance
- Individual trustee self-ratings of performance

The instrument concludes with several open-ended questions regarding members' suggestions for steps the board should take to improve each performance area.

Several other national associations have also developed tools for self-assessment by local boards. For example, the National Center for Nonprofit Boards publishes a workbook, *Self-Assessment for Nonprofit Boards* (Sleisinger, 1991), which includes questions on various dimensions of board performance. For example:

- Clarity of mission and purpose
- Evaluation and support of the executive
- How well the board monitors organization programs and services
- Performance in raising funds and managing financial resources
- Involvement in strategic planning
- New member orientations
- Board–staff relationships
- Public relations and communications with constituencies
- Risk management
- Board operations

Another useful instrument is the *Board Self-Assessment Questionnaire,* which is based on the six key competencies that distinguish highly effective boards (Chait, Holland, and Taylor, 1993). (Review these competencies in chapters 3 and 4.) The developers translated those dimensions into a self-administered questionnaire that members fill out and return for scoring and analysis (Holland, 1991). Results allow a board to identify aspects of its performance that warrant further work. Comparisons can be made between a given board's profile of scores in the six competencies and averages based on a large national sample of boards that have completed the questionnaire. This method allows a board to observe how its own performance compares with that of other boards. Benchmark findings can suggest areas the group may want to address. A copy of this tool is included in the appendix of this book.

A variety of board self-assessment tools are readily available and adaptable to local needs and circumstances. A board also can design its own self-assessment questionnaire, drawing on existing tools and its statement of goals and expectations of members. Begin this process with group discussion of key expectations of trustees, goals and purposes the board seeks to fulfill, and the ways it wants to exercise its responsibilities. Then use the list of expectation statements to create a simple questionnaire: Write each expectation as a statement and then provide space for respondents to evaluate board performance in that area over the past year. Allow a range of response options ("high, medium, low"; or "strong, moderate, weak"). Specific suggestions for improvement may be invited. A sample annual evaluation form is shown in figure 5-2.

Some boards also add questions about how the respondent would like to contribute to improving performance in any area rated low or unsatisfactory. Others focus on expectations of individual performance, asking each member to assess his or her work in each area and then to set personal goals for improvement in the coming year. The individual fills out the form and then may discuss the conclusions with others. Results serve to guide that person's efforts to become a more productive team member in the year ahead. Members may agree to discuss their conclusions openly or with a board committee charged with responsibilities for trustee evaluation and development. A sample member performance assessment is shown in figure 5-3.

A few boards extend this procedure even further to include individual growth contracts. In addition to respondent assessments of performance in each area of board expectations, there are questions such as the following:

- Do you have talents or skills in this area that the board could better utilize? If so, how?
- What specific actions can the board expect from you in this area in the coming year?

Figure 5-2. Sample Annual Board Evaluation Form

Please respond to the following questions about your views of the board of ABC Health Care. We encourage your written comments on each item. This is a confidential evaluation, and results will be reviewed by the Chairpersons of the Executive Committee and the Trusteeship Committee.

A. Board Composition and Function
   1. Do the qualifications and expertise of current members of the board provide it with the balance and range of skills needed?
   2. During the past year, have members been well informed about important aspects of board and hospital affairs?
   3. Does the board's decision-making structure work well?
   4. Is there full and open consideration of all issues at the board and committee meetings?
   5. In what ways could the board's composition and functioning be improved?

B. Attitudes and Roles of Members
   1. Have you had adequate opportunities to understand your obligations and responsibilities?
   2. Do you have adequate opportunity to know the executive and the medical staff?
   3. Do board members consistently respect the difference between policy and administration?
   4. Are members supportive of the hospital and appropriately discreet about internal matters in public?
   5. Is the board following its bylaws? If not, in what ways is it deviating?
   6. Is the orientation of new members sufficient?
   7. In what ways could the board improve the attitudes and roles of its members?

C. Board Meetings and Committees
   1. Are the board committees operating effectively? Are appropriate decisions being made at the committee and full board levels?
   2. Were your concerns addressed by the appropriate committee?
   3. Did the committee you served on function effectively with regard to
      a. Goal setting?
      b. Goal accomplishment?
      c. Conduct of meetings?
   4. Was there enough continuity (in membership and program) for your committee to be effective?
   5. Were there projects that should have been addressed by your committee but did not receive adequate attention? If so, please note those projects:
   6. Were the presentations by the administration and staff informative?
   7. Are these factors in the appropriate balance for you?
      a. Your own input of time and effort.
      b. The board's impacts on the hospital and its strength in carrying out its mission.
      c. Your personal satisfaction in your association with the hospital.
   8. In what ways could board and committee meetings be improved?

Other comments, suggestions, recommendations:

Figure 5-3. Sample Assessment of Board Member Performance

1. Please rate your service on this board over the past year in each of these areas (high/medium/low):

 a. Attend the annual board retreat and each board meeting.
 b. Make an individual contribution every year.
 c. Be actively involved in at least one committee of the board.
 d. Make three or more development contacts on behalf of the organization with corporations, foundations, planned giving programs, or individuals each year.
 e. Participate actively in at least one fund-raising event for the organization each year.
 f. Call or write our two state and three federal legislators each year on behalf of the organization and its members.
 g. Attend three or more organization functions each year.
 h. Attend at least one state, regional, or national association meeting each year.
 i. Make referrals of potential donors, volunteers, board members, committee members, and service providers.

2. In any area(s) you rated yourself low, what steps do you plan to take to improve?

3. How can the board assist you with this plan?

Please bring your plan to the meeting with the Committee on Board Development.

- What can the board or staff do to help you become more effective in this area?

Some boards charge a Committee on Board Development with conducting evaluative surveys every year or two. The survey committee meets with members to discuss their conclusions, needs, and plans for becoming more skilled team members. *Growth contracts,* then, guide a member in developing knowledge or expanding skills in order to become a more effective contributor.

Here are some other ways individuals can strengthen their performance:

- Attend governance and leadership conferences, seminars, or workshops.
- Sit in on meetings of outside similar boards.
- Rotate committee assignments.
- Serve as an understudy for a new board role for next year.
- Read the body of literature on governance and leadership development.
- Pursue other educational activities (continuing education workshops on governance, for example).

A survey committee can be instrumental in identifying ways the board can guide members in these efforts. The following examples of individual trustee growth contracts are drawn from several boards:

- Move from chairing the Program Committee to serving on the Finance Committee to learn about that area.
- Interview trustees on three system boards about their policies guiding mergers and acquisitions, and bring back recommendations on these issues to your board.
- Work with your CEO on negotiations with neighboring hospitals regarding policies for shared facilities.
- Volunteer for four or five public speaking engagements on behalf of your organization in the coming year.
- Understudy with the current board chairperson as preparation for assuming that role next year.
- Consult with three auditors and bring recommendations to the board for improving financial management performance during the next year.
- Develop a plan for expanding new trustee orientation and providing mentors for them.
- Visit three other health care boards and report on best practices in fund-raising and financial management.
- Interview trustees and identify topics for board education sessions; then identify speakers and make arrangements for three such sessions next year.
- Draft and present to the board a proposed plan for evaluating board performance (include criteria, tools, and steps).
- Meet with four other health care providers in your region and draft a proposal for improving relations between them and your board.
- Identify and evaluate potential outside resources for your next campaign and bring recommendations to the board.

Outside Assessors

Yet another approach to diagnosing board performance makes use of outside experts or consultants who collect information on the board and its work. These persons are selected for their expertise in board governance. Somewhat similar to the auditor role, they check key aspects and effects of performance, relying on interviews, focus groups, and questionnaires to collect a range of information from trustees, senior staff, and other key leaders. Assessors may contact staff, patients, sponsors, donors, community leaders, and representatives of accrediting bodies (among other sources). They may observe board and committee meetings, review reports and other documents, and interview representatives of key constituencies.

Findings and conclusions are summarized in a written report that identifies strengths and weaknesses and recommends action steps for improvement. Outside assessors often include suggestions about how other boards have dealt with a particular issue. The consultant also may give an oral presentation to the board on findings and conclusions, followed by discussion of action steps and resources for further work. Boards may engage either this or another consultant to assist with implementing recommendations.

There are several advantages to contracting an outside assessor to evaluate board performance. The consultant does the assessment work, thus saving members' time. His or her familiarity with best practices of other health care boards provides a basis for comparisons that members may not have access to. This person is less likely to miss or avoid problems that members may be reluctant to address. There is greater likelihood of candor when members talk with a neutral outsider who can probe beneath responses for further information. A consultant can raise difficult or provocative questions more easily than insiders might dare, and can separate ideas or proposals from the source, thus avoiding the impediments of old disagreements. This person can offer suggestions of ways to deal with difficult issues based on the knowledge of other boards' best practices and may also assist the group in adjusting to and working on changes.

In conclusion, all the tools and approaches to board self-assessment discussed here allow a group to examine its performance in a range of areas, identify aspects that concern members, and specify targets for improvement. Many national associations have prepared board assessment packages that can be readily adapted for local use. Boards have used them effectively to move forward in efforts to strengthen their performance. We turn now to consider some ways to apply assessment findings and implement actions for change.

Chapter 6

Holding Retreats for Board Development

Once performance improvement targets have been agreed on, board members can begin working on them. One widely used and productive means of focusing on ways to make changes that strengthen performance is a retreat.

Retreats typically are one- to two-day work sessions held away from where board meetings usually take place. Off-site retreat centers offer virtual freedom from interruptions (including telephone calls) so that sustained attention can be devoted to working on mutually identified issues. Numerous organizations hold retreats to pursue activities such as developing strategic plans, preparing for a capital campaign, addressing changes in the organization or its environment, examining challenges to mission or markets, or other organizational concerns. Here we consider the utility of retreats for helping to foster ways of enhancing board governance.

Purpose of Board Development Retreats

Governance development retreats represent not only an investment in a board's future but that of the organization it serves. Retreats provide occasions for trustees to step back from their routine business climate for a deeper look at how their board exercises its responsibilities, and how it might operate more meaningfully. For many board members, retreats have produced positive, substantial changes in performance and enabled them to use their time, energy, and resources more effectively on their organization's behalf.

Individual boards have benefited from the retreat environment to accomplish the following objectives:

- Review governance philosophies and processes.
- Rethink board roles and responsibilities.

- Reevaluate alignment of board–organization priorities.
- Sharpen member sensibilities to their organization's mission and vision.
- Assess board contributions to the organization in the context of the latter's commitment to its surrounding community.
- Identify ways to broaden value-added board guidance.

Setting aside time to establish (or reestablish) priorities, develop strategies and action plans, and evaluate (or reevaluate) time frames for expediting them reminds trustees of why they agreed to serve. A fresh look, outside the boardroom, at their function also reinforces trustee awareness of environmental changes and implications, public laws and policies, demographic and technological trends, and other factors that influence informed governance.

Retreats enhance collegiality and improve working relationships among board members and between board and staff. They have been used by many boards to explore ways the group can strengthen its own effectiveness, identify targets for change, and decide what steps to take toward achieving goals. Among the most useful guides for productive board retreats is Savage's book, *Seven Steps to a More Effective Board* (1995).

Outside facilitators have helped a number of health care boards plan and conduct retreats. By drawing on their expertise and familiarity with board dynamics, these resources bring new ideas, comparisons, and perspectives to the unique issues a board may face. As mentioned in chapter 5, a neutral outside consultant can raise difficult questions and separate ideas or suggestions from individuals (thus avoiding conflicts and disagreements among members). This person can ask provocative questions, draw attention to areas participants may have overlooked or avoided, suggest alternative approaches or solutions, push for concrete actions steps and commitments, and reinforce conclusions.

Planning the Retreat

Preparation for a board retreat should be coordinated by a work group that includes the executive, board chair and senior board members, and the retreat facilitator. This group is responsible for meeting with trustees to discern their concerns and perspectives about the board and its needs. Discussion should guide identification of purposes and objectives of the retreat, approaches to realizing them, time allocation for deliberations, and responsibilities for action plans (including time frames).

The work group may conduct an assessment of recent board performance (see chapter 5), or use already-completed assessments, to pinpoint issues to examine during the retreat. It should seek members' views on the following areas:

- The organization's present and future needs, and the board's readiness to meet them
- How well the board provides guidance to the administration
- How effectively the board addresses the organization's financial needs
- How well members understand the organization's mission and environmental trends that affect it
- Board leadership, committee structure, and meeting framework
- How well members understand their roles and responsibilities
- Whether members' time and talents are used effectively
- Board relationships and communication channels with key constituencies

These inquiries also help reveal which competencies (discussed in chapters 3 and 4) members want to address at the retreat.

Next, the group drafts a retreat agenda emphasizing three to four main issues; discussion time allotted for each one; and procedures (steps and action plans) for working on them as a team. (See figure 6-1.)

The agenda should allow enough time for reflection as well as discussion, and for eliciting the creative views of all participants. It should not feature long reports or speeches; nor should it allow the views of a few to dominate the proceedings. Agenda items should focus concisely on select issues and conclude with action plans for each issue as mutually agreed on. A draft plan is then submitted to the full board for discussion, modification, and approval. Many boards have found it useful to affirm the final plan by formal resolution and each member's commitment to remain for the duration of the retreat.

Although these preparatory steps may seem time-consuming, it is essential that the planning group include all appropriate stakeholders in efforts to target issues and formulate the retreat agenda. These steps serve the vital function of reinforcing each member's ownership of, and commitment to, the plan. Also, this approach is more promising than having one or two people "work out the plan" and announce it to the board, thereby short-circuiting others' investment in results.

Once the plan has been approved by the full board, a planning group arranges for the retreat site. Most boards favor a lodge or conference facility in a pastoral setting that allows for restful breaks and refreshing walks in natural settings. Again, the retreat site should be sufficiently remote to discourage interruptions. Ideally, it should include at least one overnight stay, with an evening devoted to a good dinner and time for trustees to socialize and become better acquainted in a non-boardroom climate, thus strengthening group cohesion.

Figure 6-1. Sample Board Retreat Plan

The Westchester Hospital board met at a rural retreat facility, beginning with lunch on Thursday at noon. Right after the meal, the Board Chairperson and the Executive Director presented an overview of the agenda and invited participants to introduce themselves and describe their expectations for the retreat.

Day 1

12:00 PM   Lunch in the Woodland Room.

 1:00 PM   Welcome, review of agenda.

Introductions: go around the room and have each participant introduce him/herself, tell his/her role on the board, what he/she does outside the board, what led him/her to accept the position as member of this board, and what his/her hopes are for this retreat.

 1:30 PM   Icebreaker exercise: Analogies.

Each board member receives two index cards; one is blank, and the other lists one of several possible analogies (and alternative views) of the board's relationship with the organization (for example, the board is to this organization as the engine is to a train). Each individual is to examine the analogy on his/her card in terms of:

• What assumptions underlie this comparison?
• How would you expect the board to behave if it accepted this view of its role?
• What would be the downside or risk associated with this approach?

The individual then decides whether to accept the offered analogy or to propose a better one. Then, she/he finds one other participant, and the pair considers the analogy preferred by each. They agree on one, find another pair, repeat the same comparison process, and conclude with an analogy preferred by the four of them. This group finds another four and repeats the process. Finally, groups of eight report their preferred analogy and their reasons for choosing it to the full group. The full group considers the proposed analogies and concludes with the one preferred by all.

 2:30 PM   Break.

Figure 6-1. (Continued)

2:45 PM   Facilitator designates several small groups to work on strategies for improving the board's performance. Each group is given the assignment of bringing back proposed answers to one of the following sets of questions. A group leader and reporter are chosen for each group.

A. What criteria should this board use to assess the value it adds to this organization? How should the board monitor and evaluate its performance? Who should provide the information, when, and by what means? Exactly what would each member be expected to do? How would the board know if the effort was successful?

B. How do board members learn how to be effective in their roles? What are the top three ways the board can improve this process? What resources will be used? Who will be responsible for what specific tasks and steps? How will the board know if the effort was successful?

C. What specific things does this board expect of its members? What criteria should be applied in evaluating the performance of each one? What information should be obtained, when, and by whom? How and to whom should the results be communicated? How will the results be used in reappointment decisions?

D. How well has this board performed over the past year as a decision-making group? What are the top three factors of the board's behavior that should be improved over the coming year? What methods should we use to ensure that the board spends its time more effectively and efficiently in the coming year? What specific steps should we take to ensure that we work well as a group? How do we monitor our progress in these areas and deal with problems?

4:00 PM   Group reports. Each group presents its conclusions and recommendations to all participants. Emphasis must be on action steps that are concrete, feasible, and assignable to a specific individual or group for implementation. Following each report, the board responds to the ideas presented and reaches some consensus about whether and how to pursue the plan presented.

5:30 PM   Social hour, followed by dinner.

8:30 PM   Evening session. Go around the room and have each individual respond to the following question: "Take a mental tour of this organization and its programs 10 years from today. What will you see then that is a result of what this board is doing (or not doing) now? Tell us exactly where you are standing; what specifically you are seeing; how it differs from the present; and what precisely the board is doing to bring about that difference."

(Continued on next page)

Figure 6-1. (Continued)

Day 2

7:00 AM   Breakfast.

8:00 AM   Facilitator designates new small groups to consider strategies for improving the board's performance. This time, each group responds to the same set of questions:

Before beginning the small group discussions, each individual is asked to write two explicit, observable, and attainable goals for the *board* for the coming year. Then, as a group, list those proposed goals and discuss them. In what areas does the group agree and/or disagree? Come to some consensus on two or three specific goals to recommend to the board. Why are these goals especially important? In what ways will the board's behavior differ if these goals are realized? How should the goals be publicized? For each goal, list the first three steps that must be taken in the coming weeks to ensure momentum. Who should undertake which task? Exactly what are the assignees expected to do? What information and resources will be needed? When will each goal be accomplished? How will the board know if the effort was successful?

9:30 AM   Break.

10:00 AM   Group reports.

Each group presents its conclusions and recommendations to everyone, followed by discussion of agreements and disagreements on goals for the full board.

11:00 AM   Make assignments for implementation. Who will do what, when, and with what resources? How will the entire board monitor progress and assess results? Conclude with an explicit plan and assignments of action steps to individuals and work groups, with dates to report results.

11:30 AM   Evaluation. Go around the room and have each member respond to the following question: "What is the most important thing you learned at this retreat?"

12:00 PM   Lunch and adjournment.

Conducting the Retreat

Once they arrive and settle in, participants should gather for a summary reminder of the key issues their work will focus on, objectives, and the schedule to be followed. Also, a brief summary of pertinent background information or alternative future directions can help set the stage for intensive work on specific group concerns. If the full board breaks into smaller discussion groups of 8 to 10, members can engage in more intensive dialogue, examining specific parts of main issues. The retreat work group should announce discussion topics in advance and formulate questions to stimulate exchange and guide the small groups.

Boards with retreat experience have made good use of prepared case studies, selected for their relevance to the board's own concerns. Case examination in small group discussions introduces participants to issues that may be adaptable to their board. An excellent resource for cases is Wood's *Nonprofit Boards and Leadership: Cases on Governance, Change, and Board–Staff Dynamics* (1996). (Chapter 10 provides three case studies on governance issues in health care organizations.) After analyzing a case and drawing generalizable lessons from it, the group then explores how conclusions apply uniquely to its board and then examines possible applications. Participants identify specific areas to be strengthened and specify goals and actions their board must take to follow through on performance improvement.

Alternatively, other boards have had small group discussions work directly on prepared questions that focus participants' attention on key issues facing the board. Combining case studies and discussion questions also works well in the retreat setting. A few examples of small group discussion questions that boards have found productive in their retreats are listed here. Additional questions appear in figure 6-2.

- What decisions and actions of this board have worked especially well? What approaches or procedures contributed to these results?
- In what specific ways does this board add value to our organization and contribute to its success? What three or four steps should the board take to broaden its effectiveness and add greater value to the organization?
- Design an educational program for this board that will enable us to develop our leadership skills and strengthen board performance. What topics, issues, and skills should be included? How should we approach each of them? What resources should we use? Who should do what, and when? How will we know if our efforts have been successful?
- What are the best indicators of how well this board is performing? What criteria should we use to evaluate our performance?

Figure 6-2. Sample Discussion Questions

- What did each committee contribute to our board's most successful decisions and actions? How were our various options identified and evaluated? What methods worked well to provide useful feedback on our efforts?

- How can this board document our most effective practices, make better use of them, and establish patterns for our future?

- What criteria should we use to monitor our performance, obtain feedback on our efforts, and assess outcomes of our action steps?

- What specific topics should be included in new member orientation and educational materials? Who should research and develop those materials? What education assessment procedures might we use?

- What clearly defined steps should we take to provide better two-way communication and improve trust between the board and each constituent (without undermining the role of senior management)?

- What steps should we take to ensure that our board determines and adheres to its long-term agenda, keeps its attention focused on priorities, and invests its time effectively and efficiently? How should we deal with attempts to amend the agenda? How should we monitor and assess our use of time and energy?

How should we collect and use information about each area? How should we apply the results?

- How well are we orienting new members? What steps should we take to strengthen their preparation and get them up to speed more quickly? Who should do what, and when?

- Who are our organization's most important constituencies—those to whom we owe attention and response? What are each constituent's expectations from this board?

- How has this board spent its time and energy over the past year? Is that allocation consistent with our strategic priorities? What are board priorities for next year?

Again, arriving at appropriate questions for retreat purposes should emerge from the board's prior assessment and trustees' discussion about their main concerns.

Small group discussions should draw each participant into working on issues and finding mutually acceptable solutions, not just listening to one or two individuals hold forth on pet ideas or preferred directions. Moderators should encourage more reticent participants to share their views and discourage the efforts of a few to dominate the procedures. Questioning old assumptions and customary practices should be encouraged, and time should be taken for brainstorming creative new approaches to issues. Groups should take time to identify a wide range of alternatives before evaluating them for feasibility. As the group starts drawing conclusions and making recommendations for action, one member should take notes on key points so as to report them back to the full board.

After discussion groups conclude their work, everyone can reconvene in plenary session, where each group's conclusions are summarized in a brief oral report to the full board. Once the board has heard and discussed these reports, it can work on overall conclusions and priorities among the various recommendations.

Then the board selects the conclusions and recommendations it agrees to work on in the coming months and develops an implementation action plan following the retreat. The plan must include three elements: allocation of responsibilities to individuals or task forces, specific results or products expected of them, and dates for reporting back to the board on progress and conclusions.

The retreat should conclude with an evaluation of its utility by all participants, and a plan for sharing the results with members who were unable to attend. Some boards use a "buddy" system to contact absent colleagues: Each trustee agrees to call a specific individual and report the actions and conclusions. In addition, a written report should summarize major conclusions, recommendations, and commitments for action. A copy of this report should be distributed to each trustee.

Board leaders must follow through with explicit application of conclusions. Doing so demonstrates their commitment to implementing the plan and modeling the follow-through expected of others.

In conclusion, the key steps in planning and conducting board development retreats stress inclusion of all trustees when identifying issues to be covered during the retreat and to engage them in asking the most important questions about those issues. The overarching purpose is to reach mutually acceptable goals for the board and clearly delineated action steps toward goal attainment. We turn now to further consideration of board goals and action steps.

Chapter 7

Setting Goals for Action

Regardless of whether work is done in a retreat environment or in the boardroom, trustees should prioritize issues and agree to concentrate on key steps toward change. Member surveys and group discussions are likely to disclose a wealth of issues and recommended actions, so many in fact that the group might become bogged down with suggestions. Rather than allowing paralysis to block forward movement, the group should list major options and then prioritize those that are feasible. Success with this initial task serves to build momentum and commitment to taking on additional challenges.

Sample Goals and Implementation Plans

Listed below are four examples of goals and implementation plans set by some boards:

- Our goal is to understand clearly and agree on board member duties and responsibilities. To accomplish that, the Committee on Trustees will draft a board members' manual, summarizing key roles and functions, and present the draft to the full board prior to our spring meeting. By then everyone will be prepared to discuss it, make revisions as needed, and vote on approval. We will then use the finalized manual to design a new member orientation program.
- Our goal is to provide clear guidance and feedback to the CEO. The Executive Committee will develop a set of objectives and expectations of the CEO role, as well as standards and procedures for evaluating that person's performance. The CEO will examine the draft plan for comment and feedback to the committee. Within six months, the committee will bring a report and recommendations on all aspects of this matter to the full board for review and approval. Then we will establish implementation procedures.

- We want to improve accessibility and utilization of all service programs. Working with senior staff, the Program Committee will oversee a consumer survey for views of our programs, hours, services, and their recommendations for improvement. The committee will prepare a report that includes specific plans for shifting resources from low-demand to high-demand areas and recommendations for improving quality in each area found to be deficient. This report will be presented to the full board prior to its meeting, which is scheduled twelve months from now. Board members will discuss the report and identify action steps for implementation.
- Our goal is to increase the level of trust throughout the organization and the community we serve. The Public Relations Task Force will work with senior administrators to review all policies on internal communication and draft specific recommendations for improvement. It will ask staff to suggest specific ways to strengthen board–staff communication and liaison. The task force also will review communications from the organization to the community, as well as channels from major community groups into the organization, and offer improvement recommendations. In nine months a report on these areas will be presented to the board for review. Based on that report, the board will set priorities for further action on this issue.

Note that each goal statement includes several essential features:

- A clear-cut group goal
- A dedicated work group to perform actions intended to accomplish the goal
- Specific action steps the group is to take
- A final product or result desired
- A time specifying when the product or result is to be presented
- Further actions to be taken

Purpose of Goals and Action Plans

By making each element explicit, those designated to carry them out understand exactly what is expected of them. Likewise, the board can monitor progress toward its targets and know when goals have been successfully attained. Examples of board goals in three other health care organizations are shown in figure 7-1.

Clearly, then, identification of a board's goals and objectives emerges from examination of key issues facing the group and group priorities.

Figure 7-1.   Examples of Board Goals in Three Organizations

Goals of Board A for the coming year:

1. Complete redrafting our guidelines for mergers and acquisitions, including full review and approval by senior staff and the board.

2. Develop and implement procedures for evaluating the board's performance.

3. Revisit the strategic plan and update as needed. Then derive from the plan the board's charges and tasks for each committee.

Goals of Board B for the coming year:

1. Develop a clear statement of goals and expectations for the position of Chief Executive Officer as well as standards and procedures for evaluating the Executive's performance.

2. Formulate a set of indicators to gauge the board's own performance as a group and develop guidelines for self-assessment.

3. Expand the diversity of this board by adding more women and minorities.

4. Come to a conclusion regarding change in board expectations for annual financial contributions by our members.

5. Plan the next board retreat, drawing upon major issues faced in the current year and expected in the next one.

Goals of Board C for next year:

1. Complete work on a Board Members' Manual, summarizing duties and expectations of all board members.

2. Implement an orientation program for all new board members and assign mentors to each.

3. Conduct two educational sessions for the board, one on reading financial statements and one on monitoring and evaluating board performance.

4. Each member will become actively involved in at least one committee.

Findings from the retreat discussions should provide a blueprint for selecting the most critical targets for attention and setting forth steps for addressing them. These targets become goals for improving the board's performance quality and enhancing its contributions to the organization in the near future. Action steps, deliverable products, and realistic time lines allow the board to monitor progress toward goal achievement. Explicit and concrete goals and action plans serve a number of functions:

- Focusing and sustaining board attention
- Providing a framework for deciding what is to be included (and excluded) from meeting discussions
- Guiding task assignments to board committees, structuring their work, and requiring reports back to the larger body

- Organizing meeting agendas
- Guiding members' expectations, energy, skills, and activities
- Facilitating progress monitoring and acknowledging successful completion of commitments

In all, these functions goals and action plans demonstrate to the whole organization how trustees intend to be accountable for resources and how they expect to show measurable performance improvements.

For maximal usefulness, goals and action plans should be made public, which puts the board on record as being committed to specified actions for which it accepts responsibility. Some boards have announced their annual goals in reports to constituencies, and then invited feedback at year's end. Others emphasize them in annual reports or feature them prominently in meeting announcements. Still others display goals prominently in the meeting room (on large posters, for example) as constant visual reminders of the group's priorities.

In monitoring progress toward stated goals, the board must also specify *how* it will know when efforts have achieved intended results. This means that the group must identify *what* constitutes successful task completion. Answers may lie in specific actions, reports, products, or observable changes to be instituted. Descriptions also should include a deadline for results and identify the individuals or work groups responsible for expediting the steps and reporting to the board. An example of one board's framework for monitoring goal progress is shown in figure 7-2.

As already noted, this system of setting goals, developing action plans, monitoring progress, and establishing outcomes measurement criteria and procedures reflects the accountability that many boards already expect of their executives. These indicators of movement, then,

Figure 7-2. Framework for Monitoring Progress on Board Goals

Goals	Action Steps	Responsibility	Report Due	Status
Goal 1:				
Goal 2:				
Goal 3:				
Goal 4:				
Goal 5:				

occur on three levels: board task group or committees, the larger board, and the entire organization.

The board must take the *time* to examine and assess information it obtains about movement toward each goal. In whatever form results are presented, the group must devote sufficient time to review them, check the evidence against expectations, and reach conclusions about their acceptability. Assigned time frames for results, reports, or other products afford a group structure for scheduling relevant discussions. The schedule should extend over a full year and allow the board to plan meeting agendas that focus on a few priorities at each session, rather than trying to hear from every committee at every meeting.

In addition to examining specific goal attainment over the course of a year, the board should step back periodically and review its overall performance more broadly. Many boards hold annual or biennial retreats for these wide-scope, comprehensive assessments, looking at movement on past goals as well as emerging issues that need attention. Some conduct broader performance assessments at these times and use findings to formulate new goals for the future in light of changing circumstances. In these ways, boards demonstrate across the organization how focused goal setting and performance monitoring lead to added value to the organization.

In conclusion, when establishing goals and action steps, some boards are highly goal focused and rigorously disciplined in working on meeting objectives—even to the exclusion of other aspects of teamwork. Other boards are concerned more with maintaining an atmosphere where everyone feels included and comfortable, even if goals are ambiguous and tasks remain incomplete. Achieving balance among all requisites of effective governance is a difficult but vital success ingredient. Boards that have settled into habit and complacency have yet to realize this equilibrium. The next chapter describes several of the boards we observed and examines how they have dealt with these matters in real practice.

Chapter 8

Examining Three Models of Governance

Boards carry out their work in many ways; no single style represents the best or only means for achieving optimal effectiveness. Most boards apply differing mixes of the six skill sets – strategic, contextual, analytical, political, educational, interpersonal – that characterize high-performance boards (as described in chapters 3 and 4). Furthermore, most demonstrate mixed styles of practicing these competencies, as dictated by local circumstances and responsibilities. Trustees should examine their work style for ways to maximize their particular strengths. One way of doing this is to observe other boards and then adapt best practices to local needs.

There may be as many board governance approaches, priorities, structures, and methods as there are boards. Generally speaking, their work patterns reflect positive values or strengths, while neglecting weaker aspects of duties and responsibilities; this leads to underperformance. Maintaining a balance of all six skill areas is crucial to effective governance.

For example, certain boards focus on maintaining harmony in interpersonal relationships (with executives and among members), while others emphasize efficient planning, task completion, and goal accomplishment – even if that emphasis sparks conflicts among players. Some boards give top priority to the external environment and focus their attention on raising funds and generating resources for the organization to carry out its mission; others are more concerned with watching internal expenditures rigorously, leaving fund-raising to the executives. Another board style emphasizes careful compliance with past commitments, policies, and organizational traditions, while its more forward-looking counterpart challenges longtime practices in the interest of innovation and experimentation around the organization's mission. Therefore, Board X may be concerned primarily with satisfying consumers, constituencies, and the community as the ultimate measure of success, while Board Y is more protective of its organization's survival and growth.

It is likely that all boards go through periods where first one style then another predominates; often the reason lies with individual trustees who infuse their own personalities, skills, and interests throughout their board's character. Although all governance models have some validity, trustees tend to fall into styles where certain values are emphasized and others are downplayed. The end result can be a one-dimensioned, stagnant board culture characterized by ineffectual performance.

High-performance boards feature diversity of skills and flexibility, that is, the capacity to adapt their approach on cue as the situation demands. These boards reject the "one-style-fits-all-issues" mind-set. Like a world-class orchestra or sports team, these boards command a repertoire of skills exercised synergistically by members selected for the individual talents they bring to group performance.

Comparing Boards along Three Dimensions

Our observations of differences in assumptions, work styles, and value orientations among boards led to identification of three basic dimensions—or profiles—along which boards may be compared:

- How boards perceive structure and authority
- How they perceive and carry out their work (duties and roles)
- How their attention is primarily focused or oriented

These dimensions provide a comparative framework for examining the various approaches boards use to carry out their governance functions.

Structure and Authority

First we consider some ways in which boards understand and deal with structure and authority. Many boards (and individual trustees) see themselves as carrying out the interests or decisions of others—whether founders, sponsors, parent corporations, or legislatures—and operating within the constraints of that outside authority. Mission and traditions of the organization, as well as past decisions exerted by others in formal leadership positions, serve to guide all current board-related actions and constrain trustees from innovations that might depart from limits circumscribed by higher authority. In this scenario, the intentions of founders or donors are the most important guides for decision making; its past legacy and commitments are the organization's major driving force.

A variation of this orientation shows up in boards that view the CEO, board chair, or executive committee as the formal authority, with the board relegated to a subordinate role. Faithful compliance with the rules or expectations of those in authority is essential to how these boards perceive their work style; seldom does a member question legitimacy of the hierarchy.

Contrast such a perspective with that of boards and trustees whose operating guideline is creative adaptation to ensure future effectiveness. They understand their functions in terms of strategic preparation for the future, their most important value being to carve out innovative alternatives that will position the organization for greater success in the years ahead. Because critical analysis, creativity, and experimentation are valued as springboards to bigger success, these groups tend to be willing to take risks and implement changes in the interest of accomplishing their organization's mission more effectively. Given that their time horizon is future focused, they view past legacies or others' decisions only as departure points, not constraints. Few participants in such boards accept past traditions or hierarchical structures as being very useful to their work.

Generally speaking, boards in this dimension fall somewhere between two extremes: dedication to past legacy and authority, *and* dedication to innovative changes geared toward the future. For a board whose trustees do not share a strong team mind-set, this fluctuation can cause conflict.

Duties and Roles

A second dimension along which boards and trustees may be examined relates to how they perceive their duties and exercise their roles and functions. Some groups, assuming that their basic responsibility is to sustain efficient and orderly movement toward explicit targets and results, identify tasks to complete, expect regular progress reports, and work to remove barriers to success. Instrumental competency and timely movement, then, are prized as strengths. For example, in reference to meetings, "Just get it done and stop talking about it!" is a common refrain among members of this persuasion.

Trustees operating along this "what-to-do-and when-to-do-it" spectrum grow impatient with anything that interferes with brisk and orderly progress toward established goals. They have low tolerance for efforts to revisit decisions or discuss alternative perspectives because these trustees want their time and energy concentrated on efficient completion of tasks, even if their colleagues disagree with the underlying conclusions.

Contrast this outlook with a board culture that values relationship harmony and group cohesion over orderly and disciplined goal attainment. These boards embrace collegiality and friendship among members and seek to avoid conflict and confrontations. Although they respect rules, laws, and policies, they see "keeping the peace" and group adaptability as bigger priorities. Because the quest for harmony overrides the search for efficient task completion, lengthy discussions, digressions, and tangential issues can overburden the deliberation process. Frequently the result is a hasty conclusion.

Again, most boards fluctuate between two extremes: relationship nurturing (accompanied by task inefficiency), *and* efficient task fulfillment (accompanied by interpersonal conflict). If both instrumental and relational competencies are not balanced among individual trustees, conflict ensues.

Attention Focus or Orientation

The third dimension along which a board's work style can be examined has to do with primary orientation and focus of board members' attention. Some boards concentrate on *internal maintenance* of their organization, that is, conserving and protecting its resources and developing the quality of its programs. These groups place high priority on building strong internal operations, within the limits of available resources. Changes in the environment or criticisms from the external community are seldom considered as useful information, because board focus is locked on internal maintenance.

Contrast this mind-set with boards whose chief concerns are *external advancement*—positive community relations and increased market share, for example. With their focus locked on strengthening the organization's competitive edge in the marketplace, they are willing to institute whatever internal changes are deemed necessary to secure a greater chunk of external resources. Feedback from outside sources and emerging regional trends, for example, are monitored carefully to identify opportunities for advancing the organization's cause and its competitive strength. Resources, whether measured in finances or community trust, are to be used as necessary to ensure organizational growth.

The two extremes along this spectrum are boards that protect the organization and its resources (to varying extents) *and* those that take calculated risks in responding to opportunities in the external environment. Differing levels of focal attention among individual trustees can cause conflicts in the board's approach to its work.

In all three dimensions, because individual board members differ in their inclinations, those at one pole may find the other's style difficult to understand or tolerate. Finding a workable balance—of skills and competencies, of mission and strategy—is the linchpin in successful governance.

In fact, the importance of balance in all these styles is highlighted by considering the extreme forms any one of them might take. For instance, rational pursuit of competitive advantage and maximum output can lead to an oppressive sweatshop atmosphere, characterized by obsession with gain, dogmatic control, and human exhaustion. Alternatively, overindulgence in comfort can lead to a complacent country club climate, where unproductive processes can breed apathy and confusion. Aggressive response to every external change can generate random experimentation, opportunism, and anarchy within the organization. Myopic attention to internal processes can make for sterile procedures and inertia. Though each approach to board work represents a valid and valuable success factor, avoiding extreme tendencies requires attention to balancing each component of the board and drawing each value into cooperation with the others (Quinn and Rohrbaugh, 1983).

Three examples illustrate alternative ways that boards deal with these performance aspects. Concerned about their performance quality, all three boards undertook improvement initiatives within the context of assumptions they made about how their board wanted to work. Each of them used the assessment questions presented in chapters 3 and 4 and designed action plans around their conclusions.

Comparisons and contrasts among these three examples—referred to here as a team of co-owners, an assembly of instrumentalists, and a booster club for the president—are instructive for understanding divergent approaches to governance as well as potential strengths and limitations of boards.

Board A: A Team of Co-Owners

Board A functioned as a team with a sense of shared responsibility and ownership of the organization. Its practice style closely approximated strength and balance among all three dimensions discussed earlier in the chapter; performance scores were high in the six competencies described in chapters 3 and 4.

Members understood the importance of clear goals that anchored group attention; at the same time, they sought to nurture positive and cohesive relationships among themselves. Members shared a deep commitment to their institution and its core values and pursued ways to adapt and reformulate them as guides for strategic planning.

Power was shared throughout the group, keeping each trustee highly involved in deliberations and decisions, and everyone regarding themselves as equal partners with one another and with their organization's leadership. They held regular educational sessions to address a range of board issues and key organizational issues, and sought performance feedback from one another, senior staff, and community leaders. Each year board members attended a retreat dedicated to examining past experiences so as to set next year's improvement goals. They also spent retreat time reviewing assessment findings. Their interpersonal skills were strong, as were their analytical and strategic competencies.

In addition to strong appreciation for their organization's mission, Board A respected its authority, as well as that of donors and sponsors; members also acknowledged the legacy of founders and past policies. They adapted past traditions, however, as guidelines for installing changes in the interest of accomplishing essential objectives to secure the organization's future. The group balanced its work emphasis on mission *and* strategy.

Board A alternated its efforts between strengthening the quality of internal programs and board processes, while at the same time paying careful attention to changes in the external environment that might pose opportunities or threats to organizational advancement. Trustees pursued the organization's mission through judicious strategic planning while also enhancing their leadership skills and interpersonal relationships with each other.

Through its shared power as a team the group emphasized board–executive partnership over a hierarchy steered by organization leaders or a board chairperson. Rigorous and critical analysis of all recommendations was valued as a means for reaching the most suitable conclusions. At the same time, members paid close attention to their collegial relationships with each other and with senior staff. Members followed trends in the environment and monitored regional and legislative developments for opportunities to advance the organization's mission.

Proposed changes and innovation were deliberated carefully before conclusions were drawn, and close attention was given to potential disruptions to staff if policy or program changes were installed. The board identified its goals through extensive group discussion and consensus rather than voting. Although they valued diverse viewpoints in seeking creative solutions, members worked toward consensus rather than moving hastily toward "win-lose through votes."

Despite being close to balance in all dimensions, this board seemed to place slightly greater emphasis on the organization's legacies and traditions than on risk taking, experimentation, or innovation. It tended not only to value internal relationships among members over efficient completion of tasks, but seemed more inclined to protect the organization than to satisfy the interests of those in the external environment. The group saw its role as providing strong, stable governance for the organization. The organization showed every indicator of successful performance, and the executive attributed much of that success to the board's effectiveness. This organization's shortcoming may be slow response to a fast-changing market.

Board B: An Assembly of Instrumentalists

Board B functioned as an assembly of "young turks"–all task-oriented instrumentalists, all strongly focused on maximizing market share. Group scores were high in the strategic and analytic competencies but low in contextual, educational, interpersonal, and political skills. Compared with Board A, this board was characterized by a much more aggressive, even opportunistic, approach to its work. Leaders were chiefly concerned with advancing the organization's competitive position by rapidly taking advantage of new opportunities in the regional market for change or expansion. Strategic planning and efficient adaptation to external opportunities were highly valued, while little was remembered of the organization's past legacy or traditions.

The health care organization governed by this board had grown rapidly in recent years and was emerging as a major and esteemed player in its region. Past ties to a founding religious denomination had been severed in a board reorganization five years earlier, at which time extensive changes in administration and board composition were introduced. By the time we came on the scene, almost all newcomers—administrative and board positions—were persons from corporate backgrounds.

These individuals believed strongly that internal operational stability could be sacrificed for changes required by new funding opportunities or innovative programs for new clusters of consumers. Current members of the Executive Committee were especially proud of the new organization and believed that the board's more aggressive approach to governance had been a crucial reason for this success. Staff other than the CEO were unavailable for comment.

Current trustees appeared to fall into two groups: a few "insiders," who were members of the Executive Committee and made most of the key decisions of (and for) the board; and "outsiders," who functioned chiefly to ratify the first group's recommendations. Strong emphasis was placed on amassing board power and status by exerting influence over resources from other organizations, and by solving problems adroitly and efficiently. Leaders compared the board to a meritocracy or oligarchy, where those with the most efficient economic power rose to positions of control; it was felt that many trustees were disdainful of any talk about inclusive group processes or cohesiveness. Changes in internal procedures of the board or of organization services were made quickly, based on Executive Committee conclusions regarding opportunities for organizational advancement. Outsiders and staff heard of these changes later and were expected either to approve or remain silent.

The board had a centralized structure for decision making, with power resting in the hands of the Executive Committee. That committee focused heavily on advancing the organization in the marketplace and was willing to make extensive, although abrupt, internal changes in operations, procedures, or past practices in order to take advantage of new opportunities. The executive was seen as an employee of the board—he might propose directions, but the board clearly was the final authority in all decisions. Dissatisfaction among staff was considered a negligible and inevitable cost of doing business and ensuring success in a demanding marketplace.

Board B made some slow measure of progress in developing strengths in neglected aspects of its performance—specifically the contextual, educational, and interpersonal competencies. These changes may not yet be sufficient for it to deal with additional problems we predict it will encounter with internal operations. Largely due to staff dissatisfaction and turnover, these problems may lead to difficulties with recruitment (although some professionals might be willing to make the accommodations required by this organization). Likewise, shifts in programs and services are likely to provoke increased community dissatisfaction and distrust, unless the board makes even greater gains in neglected competencies. We anticipate that this organization will either begin acquiring nearby hospitals to form a regional network or be bought by another network attracted to its strong financial position.

Board C: A President's Booster Club

The third governing body, Board C, functioned mainly as a booster club, or auxiliary, for the executive. Its scores were very high in the interpersonal, contextual, and political competencies, but low in educational, analytical, and strategic skills. Board C's trustees seemed to have been selected on two grounds: professional skill or a personal contact that provided a resource important to the executive, and social compatibility with other members of the group. Interpersonal relationships were strong and positive; much of the time the group functioned as a congenial social club.

Seldom were crucial issues first raised in board meetings; instead, meetings served to ratify executive decisions that emerged from private consultation with select trustees whose expertise or linkage was deemed relevant to the issue. Group structure was similar to wheel spokes, all of which radiated from a central axis, the executive. Board meetings were confined to ceremonial functions (conferring awards, honoring traditions, and preserving procedure traditions). Business sessions tended to be short, with social time before and afterward.

The executive initiated issues, recommended directions, obtained advice whenever needed, and followed through on conclusions. Trustees were called on individually to consult on issues that fell under their areas of professional expertise; however, final authority clearly resided at the executive level. In short, the president told trustees how and when they were to contribute (but privately complained of board passivity).

Board C's organization was also very successful, considered a leader among hospitals in its region. Everyone attributed this success to an executive who had held office for nearly two decades. His leadership skills, business acumen and assertiveness were praised for having pulled the organization from near extinction, upon his arrival, to a position of high esteem within the community.

Members were proud to be associated with the organization, chiefly because of its strong and successful leader. While they appeared to conduct little work as a group, individual trustees were confident that their support had contributed in important ways to the success of the organization and saw no reason to change any aspect of board operations. Only one member voiced concern about what the board would do if this executive were to leave. Meanwhile, organization and board alike show every evidence of success and satisfaction.

This example illustrates the weakness (covered temporarily by a dominant executive) that results from inattention to most duties of governance. Although interpersonal practices were strong, the board was markedly weak in its attention to mission, problem analysis, learning, and strategic planning. Some growth took place in those competencies, but unless the board strengthens itself in those areas, the organization may survive only as long as this particular executive remains. Most trustees will be unprepared to act when this person no longer runs the show, at which point the group may seek another savior to protect its past practices. If the board grows in its competencies, the organization may not depend as much on a single individual.

Concluding Analysis

All three case studies illustrate the diverse ways in which boards deal with dimensions of governance, and how board members can emphasize one or another dimension. Each board has achieved a satisfactory and productive balance (even if only temporarily) in serving their organization. Board B continues to place financial growth and increased market share well above mission, staff and community loyalty—though it has begun to pay closer attention to the interpersonal dimensions of governance. Such imbalance may well lead to staffing problems and future changes attached to merger or acquisition.

Board C continues to depend heavily on a strong executive and will face considerable difficulty whenever that person leaves, unless it hones its instrumental skills. It still has much to accomplish in developing sufficient leadership or teamwork strength for dealing effectively with succession issues, a basic responsibility of any board.

Board A was strongest in most dimensions of competence and developed even more effective teamwork among a variety of member skills and interests. It continues to provide effective leadership but may respond slowly to changes in its environment (an area to which it has begun to direct attention). Experiencing steady growth, the organization continues to enjoy loyal commitment among staff, as well as high regard in the community. In the long run, this example is the healthiest of the three and serves as a useful example of effective governance.

Chapter 9

Sustaining Ongoing Improvement Initiatives

No initiative designed to strengthen board quality and productivity should give the impression of being a quick fix or isolated action that, once completed, suggests the return to business as usual. Instead, improvements must involve fundamental and ongoing change in how the board uses its time and energy. Directing attention to the way the group currently performs and how it might enhance that performance must be incorporated continually into expectations that members have of themselves and of one another. This way, trustees build into their collective work ethic a regard for the evolutionary nature of quality improvement.

Examples of Applications

Change occurs at different rates and in different ways among boards. For example, because of its operating assumptions and work style Board A (the co-owner team described in chapter 8) assessed itself in all competency areas and identified the following improvement steps:

- Updating the organization's mission statement, applying its values and principles more conscientiously at every meeting
- Expanding board assessments of individual and group performance and using findings to plan educational sessions on a variety of topics
- Ensuring that each member be included and remain involved in important activities
- Adding time for critical analysis of key issues and taking steps to improve two-way communications with constituencies
- Sharpening the board's focus in plenary and committee meetings to concentrate on top organization priorities

In addition to these measures, this board committed to becoming stronger in each governance skill and incorporating them into ongoing practices.

The other two boards were more limited in their responses, but did effect improvement. Board B, which emphasized instrumental efficiency in its practices, found attention to strategy and analysis to be quite compatible with the group's interests; matters of context and mission, board education, and interpersonal relationships, however, were more difficult for some members to address directly. Board C, which operated as auxiliary to the CEO, grasped attention to context and mission, relationships, and communications with constituencies, but many trustees were uncomfortable with critical analysis and strategic planning. For all three groups, some assumptions that members had taken for granted were reinforced, whereas others were challenged. A few members in each group recognized the implications of underutilized competencies and actively encouraged giving attention to them, though most preferred to operate from their more familiar strengths.

To overcome resistance, leaders sought ways to incorporate correcting underdeveloped competencies into current board business, rather than addressing them in isolation from ongoing work. Beginning with their board's already-established governance skill levels and interests, leaders can gradually expand focus to other dimensions of current issues before the group and to procedures for approaching them. Over time, Boards B and C showed improvement in areas formerly neglected. Their experiences show that strengthening performance can be accomplished in a number of unobtrusive but effective ways, even if it takes time for outcomes to become evident.

Concluding Summary of Action Steps

There are many practical steps boards can take to improve their effectiveness. For example, leaders occasionally can pause after completion of work on a major agenda item and invite reflection on how they dealt with that issue and what could be done to improve the deliberation process next time. This invites attention to the group's work procedures and allows suggestion for steps to improve them. Boards also can conduct brief evaluations upon conclusion of plenary sessions and committee meetings. This presents another way of drawing the group's attention to its work habits and its commitment to ongoing improvements.

Another beneficial practice is for trustees to observe how they use meeting time and examine how their time and energy are linked to strategic priorities (rather than being consumed in tangential details). Rotating responsibility for monitoring board use of meeting time and assessing clarity of links between agenda items, discussions, and strategic commitments serves to disclose strengths and weaknesses in this area. Feedback on gaps between intentions and actual practices facilitates group efforts to change work patterns.

To sustain commitment to performance improvement, the board can charge a committee or task group (perhaps its Committee on Trustees, or the Nominating Committee) with several tasks:

- Remind the board of its commitments.
- Monitor and assess performance.
- Schedule educational workshops on deficient areas.
- Periodically present recommendations for strengthening board meeting processes.

Such a committee also can develop and implement steps for monitoring board meetings, soliciting participants' assessments and improvement recommendations, and arranging for periodic board education sessions and retreats on issues of interest.

The committee's experiences gained in carrying out these tasks will also enable it to provide useful feedback on members' contributions. It can arrange coaching sessions and mentors for underperformers and enforce term limits to ease out inadequate contributors.

Based on its experiences, the committee can provide input for new member nominations. Conclusions about strengths and weaknesses in individual skills should guide consideration of what characteristics new members should bring to the group. In terms of new member skills, boards have broadened their scope to include working with groups, improving linkages and communications with key constituencies, and showing a strong record of positive contributions to group communication and learning.

As commitment to improved performance grows, a further way to build learning into collective expectations is to schedule times and issue invitations to outside experts who can contribute in the following ways:

- Reviewing the board's performance
- Providing feedback
- Recommending aspects that need attention
- Describing best practices of other boards in relevant areas
- Conducting training sessions on specific topics or skills requested by members

Conferences and national associations are reliable resources for identifying experts and experienced leaders from other similar organizations in the region. A fresh view of itself through neutral outside eyes can yield valuable feedback and help members think more productively about areas that need attention.

In conclusion, boards can add greater value to their organizations by building into their procedures unobtrusive steps that facilitate trustees' learning from their experiences and strengthening the quality of their governance skills. By welcoming challenges confronting their organization as occasions for learning, they can conduct self-assessments to identify performance improvement opportunities. Boards can set goals and monitor progress; educate themselves about governance, the organization, and its environment; and seek to balance strengths in all competencies through effective teamwork.

Effective boards develop a culture of accountability and shared responsibility for continuous improvement of board work. In doing so, they model the accountability they expect of others throughout the organization; demonstrate priority setting; take constructive action; install performance changes that result in their added value to the organization; and prove their effectiveness as trustees who continuously earn the trust of those inside and outside the organization.

Chapter 10

Case Studies and Discussion Questions

In this concluding chapter, we present three cases and some questions to guide group examination of them. They are based on real-life governance issues faced by leaders of nonprofit health care organizations. Each case presents the reader with difficult choices, based on information provided in the text. Discussing them can help bring board attention to important issues and challenges that may have been overlooked in a board's own activities. Each case demonstrates practical applications of the concepts and principles set forth in previous chapters, and their discussion can serve as a springboard for analysis and applications in participants' own boards.

Case 1: Metropolitan Medical Center Board

Sam Lewis, President and CEO of Metropolitan Medical Center, and Fred Dickinson, Chairman of its board of trustees, were talking over lunch about how the board was performing and possible ways it might be strengthened. Metropolitan, a 600-bed hospital located on the edge of a growing urban area, owns a 125-bed nursing home. Finances are stable, and the physical plant is in good condition.

"I think we're going to face increased pressures from managed care and from large health care corporations trying to enter our market," said Sam. "And who knows what new federal and state regulations we'll encounter in the next few years. We need to think about how our board can do a better job of navigating in the stormy waters ahead."

"But we already have a good board," replied Fred. "The trustees have their hands full with overseeing our medical center board, the nursing home board, the foundation, and our community services board. As you know, we have the standard committees—executive, finance, buildings and grounds, joint conference, nominating, pastoral care, and quality assurance. Most of our members have served over 20 years and understand how to deal with all these issues. They've all done reasonably good work, so I don't see why you think we need to change."

"Well, perhaps we're a victim of our own past success," mused Sam. "There's no doubt our current structure and membership served us well in the past, and I don't mean to appear critical, it's just that things are already changing from how they were 20, even 10 years ago. For example, the population we serve is becoming younger, more minority, and more low income, yet nobody on our board knows much about these new patients—we don't even have a woman on the board, Fred! What kind of statement are we making to the community by keeping the same old guys with the same old views? If we're going to understand our community and the people we're supposed to be serving, we need some new blood."

"We'd be losing a lot of wisdom and experience by changing membership just for the sake of change," Fred replied. "After all, these guys have come through many years with the center, they know it inside-out. They trust you, they trust each other and have learned how to work together very well. I don't see how just changing actors will accomplish what you want. And it certainly will cause some disruption. There's lots to lose and little to gain, from where I sit."

"It's certainly true that our trustees have been supportive," acknowledged Sam. "But they seldom dig in and help improve recommendations that I bring to the table. They're willing to listen and raise a few questions, but the weight is all on me to come up with the ideas and the plans. They're passive-reactive, not leaders. They're no longer in touch with much of the outside world, either in government or in our patient population. Over the past few months, I've come to the disturbing conclusion that this group has no goals or criteria for assessing anything, other than how comfortable they feel with where I'm taking them. That may have been okay in the past, but I want some bright and capable partners in understanding politics and charting our course into a very unstable future. Maybe we could start by proposing some term limits and then talk about what sort of characteristics we'd like to see in new nominations. Perhaps we could also start some education sessions for trustees on encroaching changes in health care."

"I'm afraid many of them would view your efforts to change membership and expectations dimly, as a power grab," replied Fred. "A few may be ready to retire, but most are pleased with things as they are and would resist change. I'm afraid they wouldn't understand what you're trying to do. You know—'if it ain't broke, don't fix it.' Why not just leave well enough alone?"

Case 1: Discussion Questions

Use the following discussion questions to help your board analyze the Metropolitan case study.

1. What are some of the Metropolitan board's strengths and weaknesses? How would you rate this board on each of the six competencies of effective governance discussed in chapters 3 and 4?
2. How are changes in the external environment influencing expectations and demands on health care organization boards? What skills do boards need in order to govern more effectively in the future?
3. What opportunities and constraints confront Sam in moving forward on his goals for the board? How can he take advantage of opportunities and overcome constraints? What should be his short-range and long-range objectives? What resources should he draw from?
4. How would you describe Fred and Sam's relationship? What important next steps should each take in order to work together more effectively?

Case 2: Parkview Medical Center Board

As he walked down the long corridor toward the boardroom, Phil Whitehead wondered again why he kept attending these frustrating meetings. Three years ago, he had been pleased at being asked to serve on Parkview's board and looked forward to the opportunity to help make a fine medical center even stronger. How those hopes had declined since then!

Over much of his first year's service, not wanting to appear ignorant by questioning why the board performed as it did, Phil had kept a low profile. On the surface, things seemed to be going well: the hospital's budget had been balanced, admissions only slightly down, and competitors staying out of Parkview's catchment area. Only a few other trustees seemed to share Phil's concerns about the possibility of more competition in the future and how the medical center would fare in the managed care business.

Board meetings were usually efficient and carefully focused. Some committee reports were thorough, whereas others seemed vague and pointless. Everyone seemed more interested in voting to approve recommendations and moving on, rather than discussing them. Phil noted that most recommendations had few criteria for measuring success; seldom were there progress reports on task accomplishment or goals set in previous meetings. The center had an elaborate strategic plan, but the board's agenda items were rarely tied to it.

In his second year, Phil had agreed to serve on the strategic planning committee. A consulting firm had made recommendations to the medical center on developing strategic alliances with other hospitals and working with a group of high-volume primary care physicians so as to be positioned to attract more managed care business. The committee reported these recommendations, and Ben Robinson (the CEO) promised to look into them. Rather than digging in on the recommendations, the board continued to devote its energy to fund-raising, identifying new stars to serve on the board, and examining executive compensation. It seemed to Phil that most trustees assumed that, because the medical center had a strategic plan—which everyone agreed was a good one—the executive would carry it out.

The next month, Phil called Ben and asked what the center was doing with the consultants' recommendations. "We're considering them," Ben confided, "but it's difficult to carry out mergers and get the physicians aboard with what we're trying to do. I'll send you a report on our most recent steps." Phil received a huge volume containing detailed discussions of plans and projections in numerous areas. The report seemed comprehensive and detailed, but the issue was never mentioned in the following board meeting. Subsequent to that meeting, Phil said to Ben, "I'm not sure that the board understands how the plan is being implemented or how it might help with that. Could the board be more helpful in figuring out how to implement the plan?"

"Certainly the board is central to the plan," insisted Ben. "Its job is not to micro manage but to get to work raising the money so Parkview can achieve the goals detailed in the plan."

Phil agreed that the board should not be involved in micro managing, but as he walked away he wondered if a board shouldn't be involved in monitoring progress on key goals, identifying productive steps in achieving them, and helping the executive solve major problems along the way. He concluded that these activities were not taking place on Parkview's board and probably would not happen unless things changed markedly.

The next board meeting was just getting under way as Phil walked into the boardroom. "Welcome, ladies and gentlemen," boomed Ben. "We have a full agenda this afternoon, so I hope you're prepared to work a little late. In addition to our usual committee reports, we have two bids for contracts to review, a proposal for some changes in our reporting procedures, plus several budget adjustments. Then I'd like to get back to preparations for the new campaign and get that going. Any questions before we dig in?"

Phil raised his hand. "I'm not sure why we're spending our time on all these operational details, instead of keeping our focus on how the strategic plan is being implemented. For example, have we been able to form strategic alliances with other hospitals? Are we in a position to compete more effectively for more managed care business? Am I the only one who thinks we're missing some important issues?"

After a strained silence throughout the room Ben said, "Phil, perhaps we should talk about your views after the meeting. Right now, let's get working on this long list of things we already have to take care of."

Case 2: Discussion Questions

Use the following discussion questions to help your board analyze the Parkview case study.

1. What are some of the Parkview board's strengths and weaknesses? How would you rate this board on each of the six competencies of effective governance discussed in chapters 3 and 4?
2. What are some issues on this board that led to Phil's dissatisfaction? What could the board have done sooner to make Phil's participation more productive and satisfying? What could Phil have done? What should he say or do now?
3. If you were a senior trustee on this board and observed the concluding exchange, what would you do? Why? What resources could you draw on and how would you use them?
4. What were some assumptions about governance that led to the manner in which Parkview trustees handled committee assignments and used board meeting time? What are some alternative assumptions and how would they lead to different practices?
5. Based on this case study, why do some boards experience difficulty in keeping focused on strategy instead of operations? In what ways should the board be involved in strategic planning and implementation? How should such plans influence the board's work, its use of meeting time, members' talents, committee tasks, board assessment, and board accountability?
6. What goals should Parkview's board set for itself (distinct from, but leading toward, the goals it set for the hospital)? How should it implement action on each of these goals? How might it monitor progress toward these goals? How could it use the findings of such efforts to reformulate goals in the future?

Case 3: Smithville Community Hospital Board

The final case is presented in the form of a fictitious letter of resignation. The letter's author, Chris Greene, is a trustee on Smithville's board. The letter is addressed to T. J. Jones, board chair.

Dear T. J.:

As I mentioned to you last week, I am formally submitting my resignation from the hospital board and its committees. While such a step was difficult, I want to share with you my reasons for taking it.

My main reason for joining the board was to provide service to the hospital I was born in, the hospital that cared for my family over the years, the hospital whose new wing bears my parents' name. Our loyalty and devotion to the organization and its staff will never diminish. These ideals remain intact, and board service could have been one avenue for involvement.

However, several matters became such strong concerns that I felt my contributions could be better used elsewhere in our community. First, actual board meetings rarely go beyond formal votes to ratify Executive Committee decisions. Since we meet only for a few hours each quarter, there is little opportunity to engage in lively debate about the issues before us. Routine matters consume our valuable time. As I have learned, the EC meets for 1 or 2 hours immediately before the full board session and then presents its ideas and recommendations for action. This precludes effective committee work and preparation time for the rest of the trustees. I encourage you to review this model.

Second, I find that the strength of this board lies in its understanding of internal operations, as seen through the eyes of the President. I wonder how much more we need to know about the hospital, especially since many board members have not been through the facility in 3 or 4 years. Information about health care conditions in our community and nationally under managed care is absent from board deliberations. For example, last month's decision to expand the maternity ward may be appropriate, but I wonder about the expected birth rate, shorter stays, and the declining number of OBs in our community. What analysis was done, and what other options might have been considered?

Finally, as I reflect on my four years of board service, I realize that much of the first term was a learning experience for me. Perhaps I should have spoken up more often; but frequently I felt alone, with no one to turn to for answers. Silence was the result, rather than risking embarrassment at asking the "foolish" question. Probably other trustees experienced that as well.

T. J., I wish you and the board the best of luck and success in your efforts. I know you will find someone to fill this seat for the remainder of my term.

Sincerely,

Chris Greene
cc: All Board Members

Case 3: Discussion Questions

Use the following discussion questions to help your board analyze the Smithville case study.

1. How would you rate this board on the six competencies discussed in chapters 3 and 4?

2. What would it be like to serve as a trustee on this board? Why didn't Chris Greene meet his expectation of "providing service to the hospital"?

3. As a board member who received a copy of this letter, what would you do? What response, if any, should the board make to this letter?

4. What are possible alternatives for the relationship between the Executive Committee and this board? What are some advantages and disadvantages of each option? Select your preferred model and describe steps this board should take in order to institute it.

5. What is the role and function of the Nominating Committee? What could it have done in this case? What steps should this board take to create a more effective committee and more satisfied members?

6. Where does this hospital lie on the dimension from "rubber stamp" to micro management? What are some implications for the board and the top management team? What steps should each group take to improve the organizational performance *and* board performance?

Appendix

Board Self-Assessment Questionnaire

Thank you for participating in this study of nonprofit organization boards. The following statements describe a variety of possible actions by boards. Some of the statements may represent your own experiences as a member of your board, while others may not. For each of the items there are four possible choices. Please mark with a check (✓) the choice that most accurately describes your experience as a member of this board.

There are no "right" or "wrong" answers; your personal views are what is important. In order to ensure the anonymity of all responses, please do not put your name anywhere on the form. After you have completed all the items, please fold the form, insert into the envelope provided, and drop it in the mail. Thank you.

1. This board takes regular steps to keep informed about important trends in the larger environment that might affect the organization.	Strongly agree
	Agree
	Disagree
	Strongly disagree
2. I have participated in board discussions about what we should do differently as a result of a mistake the board made.	Strongly agree
	Agree
	Disagree
	Strongly disagree
3. I have had conversations with other members of this board regarding common interests we share outside this organization.	Strongly agree
	Agree
	Disagree
	Strongly disagree
4. We have had ad hoc committees or task forces co-chaired by a staff member and a board member.	Strongly agree
	Agree
	Disagree
	Strongly disagree

©Thomas P. Holland. Reproduction in any form is forbidden without the express permission of the copyright holder.

5. I have been in board meetings where it seemed that the subtleties of the issues we dealt with escaped the awareness of a number of the members.	Strongly agree
	Agree
	Disagree
	Strongly disagree
6. Our board explicitly examines the "downside" or possible pitfalls of any important decision it is about to make.	Strongly agree
	Agree
	Disagree
	Strongly disagree
7. Orientation programs for new board members specifically include a segment about the organization's history and traditions.	Strongly agree
	Agree
	Disagree
	Strongly disagree
8. This board is more involved in trying to put out fires than in preparing for the future.	Strongly agree
	Agree
	Disagree
	Strongly disagree
9. The board sets clear organizational priorities for the year ahead.	Strongly agree
	Agree
	Disagree
	Strongly disagree
10. An annual report on this board's activities is prepared and distributed publicly.	Strongly agree
	Agree
	Disagree
	Strongly disagree
11. This board communicates its decisions to all those who are affected by them.	Strongly agree
	Agree
	Disagree
	Strongly disagree
12. At least once every two years, our board has a retreat or special session to examine our performance, how well we are doing as a board.	Strongly agree
	Agree
	Disagree
	Strongly disagree
13. Many of the issues that this board deals with seem to be separate tasks, unrelated to one another.	Strongly agree
	Agree
	Disagree
	Strongly disagree

©Thomas P. Holland. Reproduction in any form is forbidden without the express permission of the copyright holder.

14. In discussing key issues, it is not unusual for someone on the board to talk about what this organization stands for and how that is related to the matter at hand.	Strongly agree	
	Agree	
	Disagree	
	Strongly disagree	
15. Values are seldom discussed explicitly at our board meetings.	Strongly agree	
	Agree	
	Disagree	
	Strongly disagree	
16. If our board thinks that an important group or constituency is likely to disagree with an action we are considering, we will make sure we learn how they feel before we actually make the decision.	Strongly agree	
	Agree	
	Disagree	
	Strongly disagree	
17. Differences of opinion in board decisions are more often settled by vote than by more discussion.	Strongly agree	
	Agree	
	Disagree	
	Strongly disagree	
18. There are individuals on this board who are identified as responsible for maintaining channels of communication with specific key community leaders.	Strongly agree	
	Agree	
	Disagree	
	Strongly disagree	
19. This board delays action until an issue becomes urgent or critical.	Strongly agree	
	Agree	
	Disagree	
	Strongly disagree	
20. This board periodically sets aside time to learn more about important issues facing organizations like the one we govern.	Strongly agree	
	Agree	
	Disagree	
	Strongly disagree	
21. I can recall an occasion when the board acknowledged its responsibility for an ill-advised decision.	Strongly agree	
	Agree	
	Disagree	
	Strongly disagree	
22. This board has formed ad hoc committees or task forces that include staff as well as board members.	Strongly agree	
	Agree	
	Disagree	
	Strongly disagree	

©Thomas P. Holland. Reproduction in any form is forbidden without the express permission of the copyright holder.

23. This board is as attentive to how it reaches conclusions as it is to what is decided.	Strongly agree	
	Agree	
	Disagree	
	Strongly disagree	
24. The decisions of this board on one issue tend to influence what we do about other issues that come before us.	Strongly agree	
	Agree	
	Disagree	
	Strongly disagree	
25. Most people on this board tend to rely on observation and informal discussions to learn about their role and responsibilities.	Strongly agree	
	Agree	
	Disagree	
	Strongly disagree	
26. I find it easy to identify the key issues that this board faces.	Strongly agree	
	Agree	
	Disagree	
	Strongly disagree	
27. When faced with an important issue, the board often "brainstorms" and tries to generate a whole list of creative approaches or solutions to the problem.	Strongly agree	
	Agree	
	Disagree	
	Strongly disagree	
28. When a new member joins this board, we make sure that someone serves as a mentor to help this person learn the ropes.	Strongly agree	
	Agree	
	Disagree	
	Strongly disagree	
29. I have been in board meetings where explicit attention was given to the concerns of the community.	Strongly agree	
	Agree	
	Disagree	
	Strongly disagree	
30. I rarely disagree openly with other members in board meetings.	Strongly agree	
	Agree	
	Disagree	
	Strongly disagree	
31. I have participated in board discussions about the effectiveness of our performance.	Strongly agree	
	Agree	
	Disagree	
	Strongly disagree	

©Thomas P. Holland. Reproduction in any form is forbidden without the express permission of the copyright holder.

32. At our board meetings, there is at least as much dialogue among members as there is between members and administrators.	Strongly agree
	Agree
	Disagree
	Strongly disagree
33. When issues come before our board, they are seldom framed in a way that enables members to see the connections between the matter at hand and the organization's overall strategy.	Strongly agree
	Agree
	Disagree
	Strongly disagree
34. I have participated in discussions with new members about the roles and responsibilities of a board member.	Strongly agree
	Agree
	Disagree
	Strongly disagree
35. This board has made a key decision that I believe to be inconsistent with the mission of this organization.	Strongly agree
	Agree
	Disagree
	Strongly disagree
36. The leadership of this board typically goes out of its way to make sure that all members have the same information on important issues.	Strongly agree
	Agree
	Disagree
	Strongly disagree
37. This board has adopted some explicit goals for itself, distinct from the goals it has for the total organization.	Strongly agree
	Agree
	Disagree
	Strongly disagree
38. The board often requests that a decision be postponed until further information can be obtained.	Strongly agree
	Agree
	Disagree
	Strongly disagree
39. The board periodically requests information on the morale of the professional staff.	Strongly agree
	Agree
	Disagree
	Strongly disagree
40. I have participated in board discussions about what we can learn from a mistake we have made.	Strongly agree
	Agree
	Disagree
	Strongly disagree

©Thomas P. Holland. Reproduction in any form is forbidden without the express permission of the copyright holder.

41. Our board meetings tend to focus more on current concerns than on preparing for the future.	Strongly agree
	Agree
	Disagree
	Strongly disagree
42. At least once a year, this board asks that the executive director articulate his/her vision for the organization's future and strategies to realize that vision.	Strongly agree
	Agree
	Disagree
	Strongly disagree
43. I have been present in board meetings where discussions of the history and mission of the organization were key factors in reaching a conclusion on a problem.	Strongly agree
	Agree
	Disagree
	Strongly disagree
44. I have never received feedback on my performance as a member of this board.	Strongly agree
	Agree
	Disagree
	Strongly disagree
45. It is apparent from the comments of some of our board members that they do not understand the mission of the organization very well.	Strongly agree
	Agree
	Disagree
	Strongly disagree
46. This board has on occasion evaded responsibility for some important issue facing the organization.	Strongly agree
	Agree
	Disagree
	Strongly disagree
47. Before reaching a decision on important issues, this board usually requests input from persons likely to be affected by the decision.	Strongly agree
	Agree
	Disagree
	Strongly disagree
48. There have been occasions where the board itself has acted in ways inconsistent with the organization's deepest values.	Strongly agree
	Agree
	Disagree
	Strongly disagree
49. This board relies on the natural emergence of leaders, rather than trying explicitly to cultivate future leaders for the board.	Strongly agree
	Agree
	Disagree
	Strongly disagree

©Thomas P. Holland. Reproduction in any form is forbidden without the express permission of the copyright holder.

50. This board often discusses where the organization should be headed five or more years into the future.	Strongly agree	
	Agree	
	Disagree	
	Strongly disagree	
51. New members are provided with a detailed explanation of this organization's mission when they join this board.	Strongly agree	
	Agree	
	Disagree	
	Strongly disagree	
52. This board does not allocate organization funds for the purpose of board education and development.	Strongly agree	
	Agree	
	Disagree	
	Strongly disagree	
53. Other board members have important information that I lack on key issues.	Strongly agree	
	Agree	
	Disagree	
	Strongly disagree	
54. Recommendations from the administration are usually accepted with little questioning in board meetings.	Strongly agree	
	Agree	
	Disagree	
	Strongly disagree	
55. At times this board has appeared unaware of the impact its decisions will have within our service community.	Strongly agree	
	Agree	
	Disagree	
	Strongly disagree	
56. Within the past year, this board has reviewed the organization's strategies for attaining its long-term goals.	Strongly agree	
	Agree	
	Disagree	
	Strongly disagree	
57. This board reviews the organization's mission at least once every five years.	Strongly agree	
	Agree	
	Disagree	
	Strongly disagree	
58. This board has conducted an explicit examination of its roles and responsibilities.	Strongly agree	
	Agree	
	Disagree	
	Strongly disagree	

©Thomas P. Holland. Reproduction in any form is forbidden without the express permission of the copyright holder.

59. I am able to speak my mind on key issues without fear that I will be ostracized by some members of this board.	Strongly agree	
	Agree	
	Disagree	
	Strongly disagree	
60. This board tries to avoid issues that are ambiguous and complicated.	Strongly agree	
	Agree	
	Disagree	
	Strongly disagree	
61. The administration rarely reports to the board on the concerns of those the organization serves.	Strongly agree	
	Agree	
	Disagree	
	Strongly disagree	
62. I have been in board meetings where the discussion focused on identifying or overcoming the organization's weaknesses.	Strongly agree	
	Agree	
	Disagree	
	Strongly disagree	
63. One of the reasons I joined this board was that I believe strongly in the values of this organization.	Strongly agree	
	Agree	
	Disagree	
	Strongly disagree	
64. This board does not recognize special events in the lives of its members.	Strongly agree	
	Agree	
	Disagree	
	Strongly disagree	
65. The board faces many policy questions that do not have clear answers.	Strongly agree	
	Agree	
	Disagree	
	Strongly disagree	
66. The board discusses events and trends in the larger environment that may present specific opportunities for this organization.	Strongly agree	
	Agree	
	Disagree	
	Strongly disagree	
67. Former members of this board have participated in special events designed to convey to new members the organization's history and values.	Strongly agree	
	Agree	
	Disagree	
	Strongly disagree	

©Thomas P. Holland. Reproduction in any form is forbidden without the express permission of the copyright holder.

68. This board provides biographical information that helps members get to know one another better.	Strongly agree	
	Agree	
	Disagree	
	Strongly disagree	
69. This board seeks information and advice from leaders of other similar organizations.	Strongly agree	
	Agree	
	Disagree	
	Strongly disagree	
70. This board makes explicit use of the long-range priorities of this organization in dealing with current issues.	Strongly agree	
	Agree	
	Disagree	
	Strongly disagree	
71. This board understands the norms of the professions working in this organization.	Strongly agree	
	Agree	
	Disagree	
	Strongly disagree	
72. Members of this board seldom attend social events sponsored by this organization.	Strongly agree	
	Agree	
	Disagree	
	Strongly disagree	
73. More than half of this board's time is spent in discussions of issues of importance to the organization's long-range future.	Strongly agree	
	Agree	
	Disagree	
	Strongly disagree	

Source: Kellogg Project on Effective Governance. Adapted from form originally developed by the Center for Higher Education Governance and Leadership, University of Maryland, College Park, under funding by the Lilly Endowment, 1991. ©Thomas P. Holland. Reproduction in any form is forbidden without the express permission of copyright holder.

Reference List

Abendshien, J. *A Guide to the Board's Role in Strategic Business Planning.* Chicago: American Hospital Publishing, 1988.

Alexander, J. A. Governance for whom? The dilemmas of change and effectiveness in hospital boards. *Frontiers in Health Services Management* 6(3):38–46, Spring 1990a.

Alexander, J. A. The changing character of hospital governance. Report from Hospital Research and Educational Trust/American Hospital Association, Chicago, 1990b.

Alexander, J. A., and Morlock, L. L. CEO–board relationships under hospital corporate restructuring. *Hospital and Health Services Administration* 33(4):435–48, Winter 1988.

Alexander, J. A., and Schroer, K. A. Governance in multi-hospital systems: an assessment of decision making responsibility. *Hospital and Health Services Administration* 30(2):9–20, Summer 1985.

American College of Healthcare Executives. *Contracts for Healthcare Executives.* 3rd ed. Chicago: ACHE, 1995.

American Hospital Association. *Guidelines: Physician Involvement in Governance of Health Care Institutions.* Chicago: AHA, 1982.

American Hospital Association. *Guidelines: Role and Functions of the Hospital Governing Board.* Chicago: AHA, 1982.

Association of Governing Boards of Colleges and Universities. *Recommendations for Improving Trustee Selection.* Washington, DC: AGBCU, 1980.

Association of Governing Boards of Colleges and Universities. *Self-Study Criteria for Governing Boards of Independent Colleges and Universities.* Washington, DC: AGBCU, 1986.

Bader, B. S. *Informing the Board About Executive Performance and Compensation.* Rockville, MD: Bader and Associates, 1991a.

Bader, B. S. *Informing the Board About Finances.* Rockville, MD: Bader and Associates, 1991b.

Bader, B. S. *Informing the Board About Medical Staff Credentialing and Development.* Rockville, MD: Bader and Associates, 1991c.

Bader, B. S. *Informing the Board About Mission and Strategic Planning.* Rockville, MD: Bader and Associates, 1991d.

Bader, B. S. *Informing the Board About Quality.* Rockville, MD: Bader and Associates, 1991e.

Bader, B. S. *Keys to Better Governance Through Better Information.* Rockville, MD: Bader and Associates, 1991f.

Bader, B. S. *Rediscovering Quality: What Healthcare Leaders and Managers Need to Know About the Total Quality Transformation.* Rockville, MD: Bader and Associates, 1992.

Balda, J. B. The liability of nonprofits to donors. *Nonprofit Management and Leadership* 5(1):67–83, Fall 1994.

Bley, C. M., and Shimko, C. T. *A Guide to the Board's Role in Hospital Finance.* Chicago: American Hospital Publishing, 1987.

Bowen, W. G. *Inside the Boardroom.* New York City: John Wiley and Sons, 1994.

Bradford, C. K., and Tiscornia, J. F. *Monitoring the Hospital's Financial Health.* Chicago: American Hospital Publishing, 1987.

Burdett, R. J. *Director Liability: A Guide to Preventing Trouble in the Hospital Boardroom.* Chicago: American Hospital Publishing, 1991.

Carver, J. *Boards That Make a Difference: A New Design for Leadership in Nonprofit and Public Organizations.* San Francisco: Jossey-Bass, 1991.

Chait, R. P. *The New Activism of Corporate Boards and the Implications for Camus Governance.* Washington, DC: Association of Governing Boards of Universities and Colleges, 1994.

Chait, R. P., Holland, T. P., and Taylor, B. E. *Improving Board Performance.* Phoenix, AR: Oryx Press, 1996.

Chait, R. P., Holland, T. P., and Taylor, B. E. *The Effective Board of Trustees.* Phoenix, AR: Oryx Press, 1993.

Chait, R. P., and Taylor, B. E. Charting the territory of nonprofit boards. *Harvard Business Review* 7(1):44–54, Jan. 1989.

Coopers and Lybrand. *Audit Committee Guide.* New York City: Coopers and Lybrand (no date given).

Delbecq, A. L., and Gill, S. L. Developing strategic directions for governing boards. *Hospital and Health Services Administration* 33(1):25–35, Spring 1988.

Drucker, P. F. Lessons for successful nonprofit governance. *Nonprofit Management and Leadership* 1(1):7–14, Fall 1990.

Ewell, C. M. Should we pay hospital boards? *Trustee* 42(3):21, 26, Mar. 1989.

Faerman, S. R., and Quinn, R. E. Effectiveness: the perspective from organization theory. *The Review of Higher Education* 9:13–23, Sept. 1985.

Fink, G., and Grant, R. E. Justifying reasonable compensation. *Trustee* 45(12):21, Dec. 1992.

Fry, R. E. Accountability in organizational life: problem or opportunity for nonprofits? *Nonprofit Management and Leadership* 6(2), Winter 1995.

The Governance Institute. *Incentive Compensation for CEOs: Current Practices and Trends for the Future.* La Jolla, CA: The Governance Institute, 1990b.

The Governance Institute. *Involving Physicians in Capital Spending Decisions.* La Jolla, CA: The Governance Institute, 1991a.

The Governance Institute. *Issues in CEO Performance Appraisal.* La Jolla, CA: The Governance Institute, 1991b.

The Governance Institute. *Prudent Investment of Hospital Funds: A Senior Management/Governance Perspective.* La Jolla, CA: The Governance Institute, 1992.

The Governance Institute. *The Board's Role in Approving Physicians: Using Financial Factors.* La Jolla, CA: The Governance Institute, 1991c.

The Governance Institute. *What Does a Good CEO Cost?* La Jolla, CA: The Governance Institute, 1990a.

Greenleaf, R. K. *Servant Leadership.* New York City: Paulist Press, 1977.

Griffith, J. R. *The Well Managed Community Hospital.* Ann Arbor, MI: Health Administration Press, 1992.

Griffith, J. R. Voluntary hospitals: are trustees the solution? *Hospital and Health Services Administration* 33(3):295–310, Fall 1988.

Hageman, W. M., and Umbdenstock, R. J. Organizing and focusing the board's work: keys to effectiveness. *Frontiers of Health Services Management* 6(3):29–46, Spring 1990.

Heidrick and Struggles, Inc. *The Changing Board.* Chicago: Heidrick and Struggles, Inc., 1990.

Herzlinger, R. E., and Krasker, W. Who profits from nonprofits? *Harvard Business Review* 65(1):93–106, Jan.–Feb. 1987.

Holland, T. P. Self-assessment by nonprofit boards. *Nonprofit Management and Leadership* 2(1):25–36, Fall 1991.

Holland, T. P., Chait, R. P., and Taylor, B. E. Board effectiveness: identifying and measuring trustee competencies. *Journal of Research in Higher Education* 30(4):435–53, Oct. 1989.

Hospital Trustees of New York State. *The Trustee Handbook.* New York City: Hospital Trustees of New York State, 1988.

Houle, C. O. *Governing Boards: Their Nature and Nurture.* San Francisco: Jossey-Bass, 1989.

Joint Commission on Accreditation of Healthcare Organizations. *Accreditation Manual for Hospitals.* Oakbrook Terrace, IL: JCAHO, 1992.

Jordan, L. R. Strong, effective boards: a necessity for the '90s. *Frontiers of Health Services Management* 6(3):34–37, Spring 1990.

Keiffer, M. What the board should expect from an executive search firm. *Trustee* 42(11):28, Nov. 1989.

Kenny, D. E., and Meyer, L. L. The board's role in major transactions. *Trustee* 42(5):12, May 1989.

Kovner, A. R. Improving hospital board effectiveness: an update. *Frontiers of Health Services Management* 6(3):3–27, Spring 1990.

McComb, J. P. *Governing Community Hospitals: A Primer for Trustees and Health Care Executives.* San Francisco: Jossey-Bass, 1992.

Molinari, C., Morlock, L., Alexander, J., and Lyles, C. A. Hospital board effectiveness: relationship between board training and hospital financial viability. *Healthcare Management Review* 17(3):43–49, Summer 1992.

Munitz, B., and Neff, C. B. *The Business of Presidential Search.* Washington, DC: Association of Governing Boards of Universities and Colleges, 1990.

Orlikoff, J. E. Preventing malpractice: the board's role in risk management. *Trustee* 44(9):8–9, 19, Sept. 1991.

Orlikoff, J. E. *Quality from the Top: Working with Hospital Governing Boards to Assure Quality.* Chicago: Pluribus Press, 1990a.

Orlikoff, J. E. What every trustee should know about D&O liability. *Trustee* 43(1):8, 9, Jan. 1990b.

Orlikoff, J. E., and Totten, M. K. *The Board's Role in Quality Care: A Practical Guide for Hospital Trustees.* Chicago: American Hospital Publishing, 1991.

Pointer, D. D., and Ewell, C. M. *Really Governing: How Health System and Hospital Boards Can Make More of a Difference.* New York City: Delmar, 1994.

Pound, J. The promise of the governed corporation. *Harvard Business Review* 71(2):89–98, Mar.–Apr. 1993.

Quinn, R. E., and Rohrbaugh, J. A spatial model of effectiveness criteria: toward a competing values approach to organizational analysis. *Management Science* 29:363–77, Dec. 1983.

Rindler, M. *The Challenge of Hospital Governance: How to Become an Exemplary Board.* Chicago: American Hospital Publishing, 1992.

Ritvo, R. A. Organizational adaptation to environmental change: the hospital board's role. *Hospital and Health Services Administration* 25(1):23–37, Winter 1980.

Ritvo, R. A. The role of governing boards of trustees in promoting total quality management. *American Journal of Medical Quality* 8(2):97–102, Summer 1993.

Rosenberg, C. E. *The Care of Strangers: The Rise of America's Hospital System.* New York City: Basic Books, 1987.

Savage, T. J. *Seven Steps to a More Effective Board.* Rockville, MD: The Cheswick Center, 1995.

Schein, E. H. How can organizations learn faster? The challenge of entering the green room. *Sloan Management Review* 34(2):85–92, Winter 1993.

Senge, P. *The Fifth Discipline: The Art and Practice of the Learning Organization.* New York City: Doubleday/Currency, 1990.

Senge, P., Kleiner, A., Roberts, C., and others. *The Fifth Discipline Fieldbook: Strategies and Tools for Building a Learning Organization.* New York City: Doubleday/Currency, 1994.

Shortell, S. M. New directions in hospital governance. *Hospital and Health Services Administration* 34(1):7–23, Spring 1989.

Shortell, S. M. *Strategic Choices for America's Hospitals: Managing Change in Turbulent Times.* San Francisco: Jossey-Bass, 1990.

Sleisinger, L. *Self-Assessment for Nonprofit Boards.* Washington, DC: National Center for Nonprofit Boards, 1991.

Smith, D. H. *Entrusted: The Moral Responsibilities of Trusteeship.* Bloomington, IN: Indiana University Press, 1995.

Sofaer, S. What do we really know about the impact of boards on nonprofit hospital performance? *Journal of Health Administration Education* 9(4):425–42, Fall 1991.

Starkweather, D. Hospital board power. *Health Services Management Research* 1(2):74–86, Summer 1988.

Starr, P. *The Social Transformation of American Medicine: The Rise of a Great Profession and the Making of a Vast Industry.* New York City: Basic Books, 1982.

Stephens, R. *In Sickness and in Wealth: America's Hospitals in the Twentieth Century.* New York City: Basic Books, 1989.

Taylor, B. E., Chait, R. P., and Holland, T. P. The new work of the nonprofit board. *Harvard Business Review* 74(5):36–47, Sept.–Oct. 1996.

Umbdenstock, R. J. *So You're on the Hospital Board.* Chicago: American Hospital Publishing, 1992.

Umbdenstock, R. J., and Hageman, W. M. *Critical Reading for Hospital Trustees.* Chicago: American Hospital Publishing, 1991.

Umbdenstock, R. J., and Hageman, W. M. *Hospital Corporate Leadership: The Board and Chief Executive Officer Relationship.* Chicago: American Hospital Publishing, 1984.

Umbdenstock, R. J., and Hageman, W. M. The five critical areas for effective hospital governance of not-for-profit hospitals. *Hospital and Health Services Administration* 35(4):481–92, Winter 1990.

Witt, J. A. *Building a Better Hospital Board.* Chicago: Health Administration Press, 1987.

Wood, M. M., editor. *Nonprofit Boards and Leadership: Cases on Governance, Change, and Board–Staff Dynamics.* San Francisco: Jossey-Bass, 1996.

Index

Accountability of board, 4, 12–13
Action plans, 60–63. *See also* Goals and
    goal setting
Administration versus governance, 4
Agendas
    for board meetings, 20–21
    for board member retreats, 52–54
Analytical dimension of competency,
    25–28
Assessment of board performance,
    39–47
    and end-of-meeting feedback, 39–40
    by outside assessors, 46–47
    self-assessment, 14, 35–36, 40–45
    questionnaire for, 87–95
Association of Governing Boards, 2

Board meetings
    consent agendas for, 20–21
    and effective use of meeting time, 13,
        14, 20, 76
Board member retreats, 49–57
    conducting, 55–57
    evaluation of, 57
    facilitators for, 50
    preparation and planning for, 50–51
    purpose of, 49–50
    sample agenda for, 52–54
    small group discussions during,
        55–57
Board members
    CEO as voting, 34–35
    dissatisfied, 13–14
    diversity of, 26
    insights of new, 6–7, 11
    motivations of, 3

    orientation of new, 23
    philosophies of, 3
    selection of new, 4
    training of new, 6, 31–32
Board Self-Assessment Questionnaire, 43,
    87–95
Boards
    accountability of, 4, 12–13
    adherence to structure and authority
        by, 66–67
    as assembly of instrumentalists, 70–72
    assessment of performance, 39–47
        and end-of-meeting feedback, 39–40
        by outside assessors, 46–47
        self-assessment, 14, 35–36, 40–45
        questionnaire for, 87–95
    case studies of, 79–85
    changing customs of, 4
    competencies of
        analytical, 25–28
        contextual, 23–25
        dimensions of, 17–18
        educational, 31–34
        and governance, 65
        instrumental, 17–28
        interpersonal, 34–37
        political, 29–31
        social, 17–18, 29–37
        strategic, 18–22
    as co-owners, 69–70
    external advancement of, 68
    failures of many, 5–6
    focus of attention of, 3, 68–69
    functions of, 5
    impact of, on organizational manage-
        ment, 3

(continued)

Boards *(continued)*
  improvement initiatives for, 75–78
  increasing performance levels of, 9–10
  internal maintenance of, 68
  issues affecting effectiveness of, 1–4
  need for diverse representation on,
    26
  perception of duties and roles by,
    67–68
  as president's booster club, 72–73
  reexamination of role of, 10
  responsibilities of, 4–7
  team development of, 2–3
Bowen, W. G., 2
Bylaws and meeting requirements, 20

Carver, John, 2
CEO (Chief Executive Officer)
  commitment of to improvement of
    board performance, 15
  overdependence on, 72–73
  as partner of board, 35
  selection of, 5
  as voting member of board, 34–35
Chait, R. P., 17, 23, 43
Committees of boards, 5, 6
  clinical staff leaders on, 22
  education, 32
  executive, 84
  finance, 5
  nominating, 34, 36
  planning, 5
  survey, 46
Confrontations with key constituents,
  10
Consent agenda, 20–21
Constrictive rules, changing, 20
Contextual dimension of competency,
  23–25
Cost controls, corporate demands for, 1

Discontent, channeling, 13–14
Dissatisfaction
  of key constituents, 10
  as means to improve board perfor-
    mance, 13–14

Education committee, 32
Educational dimension of competency,
  31–34

Ewell, C. M., 42
Executive committee, 84
External environmental trends, 19

Feedback, end-of-meeting, 39–40
Finance committee, 5
For-profit health care organizations,
  burdens placed on, 1–2
Future, need to focus on, 19

Goals and goal setting, 59–63
  monitoring progress toward, 62–63
  need to review, 63
  publicizing annual, 62
  purpose of, 60–63
  sample, 59–61
Governance
  versus administration, 4
  dimensions of, 66–69
  models of, 65–73
  signs of less effective, 6
Governance Institute, 42
Growth contracts, 43, 45

Health maintenance organizations, 1
Holland, T. P., 17, 21, 23, 43
Houle, C. O., 2

Implementation plans, 59–61
Instrumental competencies, 17–18
  analytical dimension of, 25–28
  contextual dimension of, 23–25
  strategic dimension of, 18–22
Internal strengths and limitations, 19
Interpersonal dimension of competency,
  34–37
Issues, contributory, 10

Joint Commission on Accreditation of
  Healthcare Organizations
  (JCAHO), standards for gover-
  nance boards of, 40, 42

Leadership
  in creating a learning organization,
    15–16
  transitions in, 11

Learning organizations
and educational competency, 31
leadership in creating, 15–16

Managed care, 1
Management, partnership with governing board and, 3
Mission and mission statement
and changes in direction, 23
focusing on, 3

National Center for Nonprofit Boards,
42
Natural events, taking advantage of,
10–12
New England Healthcare Assembly, 2
Nominating committee, 34, 36
*Nonprofit Boards and Leadership: Cases
on Governance, Change, and
Board–Staff Dynamics* (Wood),
55

Organization, turning points in, 10
Organizational management, impact of
boards on, 3

Partnerships
between board and CEO, 15, 35
between board and management, 3
between board members, 35
Performance improvement
assessing performance level and identifying targets for change,
39–47
building instrumental competencies,
17–28
building social competencies, 29–37
case studies in, 79–85
examining models of governance,
65–73
getting started on, 1–8
holding retreats for, 49–57
initial steps toward making changes,
9–16
self-assessment questionnaire for,
87–95
setting goals for action, 59–63

sustaining ongoing improvement
initiatives, 75–78
Philosophies of board members, 3
Planning committee, 5
Pointer, D. D., 42
Political dimension of competency,
29–31
Public policy, changes in, 1, 23
Public trust, 4

Quinn, R. E., 69

Rohrbaugh, J. A., 69

Savage, T. J., 50
Self-assessment questions in channeling
discontent, 13
Self-evaluation tools, 40–46
Seminars and workshops for board
members, 32
Senge, Peter, 16, 31
Sleisinger, L., 42
Social competencies, 17–18, 29
educational dimension of, 31–34
interpersonal dimension of, 34–37
political dimension of, 29–31
Social events and board partnerships,
35
Strategic dimension of competency,
18–22
Strategic planning
consequence of neglecting, 20
process of, 18–19
Survey committee, 46

Taylor, B. E., 17, 23, 43
Teams, boards as, 2–3
Transitions in leadership, 11
Trends assessment, 19
Trustees. See Board members

Umbdenstock, R. J., 5

Whole group attention, 13
Wood, M. M., 55